The Curse of the Rainbow Jersey

THE
CURSE
OF THE
RAINBOW
JERSEY

Cycling's Most Infamous Superstition

Graham Healy

BREAKAWAY BOOKS
HALCOTTSVILLE, NEW YORK
2013

ISBN: 978-1-62124-001-3
Library of Congress Control Number: 2013932928

Published by Breakaway Books
P.O. Box 24
Halcottsville, NY 12438
www.breakawaybooks.com

FIRST EDITION

Contents

Acknowledgments

This book would have been impossible to complete without the great help of a number of people. First, I would like to thank my wife, Nina, for her ongoing support and patience during this process.

For their valuable input and feedback, I would like to thank John Marron, my brother David, Richard Rosenthal, David Gill, and Karen Larsen. I'd also like to thank my parents, Paddy and Margaret.

Lastly, I would like to thank Garth Battista at Breakaway Books for his support and his faith in this book.

Prologue

The Giro di Lombardia, or the Race of the Falling Leaves as it is often known, is traditionally one of the first races where newly crowned World Road Race Champions can show off their recently acquired rainbow jersey. Photographers gather around at the start to get one of the first shots of the jersey with the team logos printed on.

In September 2012, the Belgian cyclist Philippe Gilbert was the man who garnered most attention from journalists and photographers alike at the start of the race in Bergamo. He had captured the world title just a week previously in Valkenburg in the Netherlands, and his emphatic win that day had made him the clear favorite to add the Italian classic to his ever-growing palmarès. Having not raced since his triumph, Lombardy was his first appearance in the rainbow jersey. Prior to the race, the likable Gilbert had spoken to reporters: "It will be a bit special as it will be the first time I will wear this jersey," he said. "I just received it today at the hotel. They did good work, actually, it is looking nice with the BMC logo on it."

Forecasters had predicted heavy rain for the day of the race, which would likely make for slippery and dangerous conditions, but this didn't seem to bother a confident Gilbert; he felt that it would even play into his hands. "It is very good for me as I am very good in the descents, and I have the best tires in the market," he told the press beforehand.

The first few hours of the race went to plan for the new World Champion, who stayed with the main group, which was being whittled down to just sixty riders. However, with eighty kilometers remaining in the race—as he was chasing to catch the leaders, having been tailed off on the climb of the Muro di Sormano—it all came unstuck. Prior to the race, some commentators had decreed the inclusion of this climb after an absence of fifty years to be an act of lunacy by the organizers. The Muro had previously been used in the race in the early 1960s but was discontinued due to riders having to dismount and walk up.

It was now felt by many observers that the ridiculously steep gradients of up to 27 percent, combined with torrential rain, would cause chaos on the descent. They predicted correctly. As the riders descended, a number slid to the ground, including Gilbert in his dirt-stained rainbow jersey. He had won in Lombardy in both 2009 and 2010, but now his race was over, as he climbed into his team car shortly afterward.

In the days following the incident, Gilbert was asked the same question by numerous journalists. Did he believe he was another victim of "the curse of the rainbow jersey"? The new World Champion sounded somewhat unsure, replying, "I hope not. I don't believe in it." He went on to provide his own explanation for why previous champions had struggled: "I think this is also because the World Champion is demanded everywhere. When you are not serious in the winter, then you have a bad season. Maybe that is why the rainbow jersey can have problems."

He told reporters that despite not crashing very often, he didn't put the blame for his crash in Lombardy on the curse. Gilbert was facing the same perennial line of questioning that every World Champion had faced for the past few decades. Cycling fans can now expect this question to crop up as soon as the first piece of bad luck happens to the new wearer of the jersey, no matter how innocuous that bad luck is.

The 2012 World Champion Philippe Gilbert crashes
in the Giro di Lombardia shortly after taking the world title.

While most people—including myself—would have absolutely no belief in a particular piece of sports clothing being cursed, I did want to look at whether there is a correlation between winning the rainbow jersey and a downturn in riders' performance—and, if so, the reasons why this is happening. This book also offered the opportunity to look at other superstitions that some professional cyclists and other sportspeople believe in, and how this may affect their performance. Some of these superstitions may appear absolutely irrational to most people, but it's clear that they can create a negative thought process within the minds of athletes.

I have recounted stories of particular wearers of the jersey, and the bad luck or even tragic misfortune that befell them while wearing the rainbow colors, and have tried to determine whether there is anything to substantiate the myth. Researching the book also proved to be revealing with regard to the career and personal difficulties that some World Champions endure. Moreover, it's not just cycling that has superstitions associated with it; other sports also do, and many of these supposed curses are a lot more bizarre than a cursed jersey.

1

The Worlds

One of the strange things about the sport of cycling is that the World Championships isn't the most prestigious or best-known race. A lot of sports fans with a passing interest in cycling know the winner of the Tour de France each year, but not who the World Champion is. The World Championships Road Race can also be a strange event. Given its title, it would suggest that the best rider in the world should prevail, but the race is often won by relatively unknown riders. In turn, some of the best cyclists in the history of the sport never claimed the title. Riders of the caliber of Jacques Anquetil, Sean Kelly, and Miguel Indurain could never call themselves the World Road Race Champion.

Apart from its name being something of a misnomer, the World Championships has a number of other features that make it unique. The championships could be considered a relatively new race compared with some of the one-day classics. The first Paris–Roubaix was held in 1896; Liège–Bastogne–Liège is even older, having been first run in 1892, as a means of publicizing the newspaper *L'Expresse*. By comparison, the first World Championships wasn't held until 1927.

Other race organizers in the past had called their events the

World Championships, but this was the first road event run under the auspices of the Union Cycliste Internationale. The UCI is the governing body for cycling worldwide and had been formed in 1900 in Paris.

In 1889, British cycling race organizers promoted a one-hundred-mile time trial that they called the World Championships, which set a trend for other countries to run events with equally impressive titles. The UCI's predecessor, the ICA (International Cycling Association), had organized what could be called the first genuine World Championships for track cycling as far back as 1893 in Chicago.

In 1922, the first Grand Prix Wolber was run in France, and it was considered an unofficial World Road Race Championships. It was an invite-only race, with only podium finishers from the top events in France, Belgium, Italy, and Switzerland being invited. It was won by the likes of Francis Pélissier, Georges Ronsse, and Costante Girardengo. Around the same time, Italian race organizers ran a World Championship series of races. The UCI recognized that the time was right to arrange a World Road Race Championships.

The first championship was held at the Nürburgring motor racing circuit. The track at the Nürburgring had only opened in the spring of 1922, and the World Cycling Championships were held on June 19, one month before the first German Grand Prix took place at the venue.

A total of forty-five riders, including seventeen professionals, lined up to face 184 kilometers. The race was won by Alfredo Binda, who led a clean sweep of the places for Italy, as their four-man team filled the top four positions. It still remains the only championship where just one country has taken all of the podium places.

Binda finished 7:15 ahead of Costante Girardengo. Binda had won the Giro d'Italia earlier that season in emphatic style. His climbing ability suited the hilly circuit, which had been built in the Eifel Mountains. What was of most concern to the UCI, though, was the fact that the Belgian Jean Aerts had finished in fifth. Their unease was due to Aerts being an amateur. It reflected badly on the professionals in the race that they were beaten by an amateur. The following year would see the UCI organize both professional and amateur World Championships.

The organizers presented Binda with a jersey that he would be entitled to wear until the next World Championships. The jersey was white with blue, red, black, yellow, and green bands around the center. It was felt that this rainbow-colored jersey would make it easier for spectators to spot the World Champion; on the flip side, it also made it easy for competitors to spot the title holder.

The colors of the bands were the same as those used in the Olympic symbol. The founder of the modern Olympics, Baron Pierre de Coubertin, had designed the symbol in 1912, and it was used on the Olympic flag for the 1920 games in Antwerp. Coubertin later explained the rationale behind his five-ringed design: "The six colors [including the flag's white background] thus combined reproduce the colors of all the nations, with no exception. The blue and yellow of Sweden, the blue and white of Greece, the tricolors of France, England and America, Germany, Belgium, Italy, Hungary, the yellow and red of Spain next to the novelties of Brazil or Australia, with old Japan and new China. Here is truly an international symbol."

In 1934, Karel Kaers became the youngest-ever winner of the title in Leipzig, but the event is not so much remembered for this achievement as it is for the menacing sight of four thousand Nazi brownshirts marshaling the circuit. At the sprint at the end, one of Kaers's teammates, Gus Daneels, deliberately blocked the previous year's winner, Learco Guerra, enabling his compatriot to win. The Italian was livid, and, sensing this, Daneels rode straight back to his hotel, barricading himself in his room for the night, as he feared retribution.

One of the unique aspects of the World Road Race Championships that differentiates it from the other great one-day races is that it is held in a different country each year, and the courses vary annually. Paris–Roubaix or Milan–San Remo, for example, might have slight adjustments from one running of the race to the next, but they are fundamentally the same race. The Worlds, on the other hand, has been held in differing locations across the globe. These locations vary from the high altitudes of the Andes to low-level courses in Denmark and the Netherlands; from urban courses in Montreal to motor racing circuits in Germany; and from courses in the Alps suited to climbers, to flat courses designed for sprinters.

The World Championships has been the scene of many other controversies over the years. The fact that it's the only race of the season where riders compete for their countries rather than for their trade teams has helped create many of these controversial episodes. Managers of various nations down through the years have found it can be quite a challenging task bringing some big egos together on the same team. It doesn't always work, and there have been countless occasions of so-called teammates racing against each other.

Cycling fans didn't have to wait long for the first instance of discontent within a team camp—it came, as it happened, at just the second-ever hosting of the event in 1928. The Belgian Georges Ronsse took advantage of infighting within the Italian team to win by nearly twenty minutes. The two Italian stars of the day, previous winner Alfredo Binda and Costante Girardengo, both ended up abandoning the race. This did not go down well with the Italian federation, which suspended the pair for six months. The official statement from the federation read that the reason was "for not having defended with faith and determination the prestige of Italian cycle sport."

History would repeat itself two decades later when the two Italian idols of the time, Fausto Coppi and Gino Bartali, would also invoke the wrath of the Italian federation. The duo quit the race in Valkenburg in Holland after both riders stubbornly refused to chase any riders who had attacked. The communiqué from the Italian federation issued after the race stated, "In the World Championships they have forgotten to honor the Italian prestige that they represent. Thinking only of their personal rivalry, they abandoned the race, to the approbation of all sportsmen." They were both also given suspensions, this time for three months.

Personal feuds have also arisen at the World Championships. In 1966 two Frenchmen, Jacques Anquetil and Raymond Poulidor, found themselves in the winning break being held at the Nürburgring motor racing circuit. The two should have worked well together to ensure a French win, as they had dropped the German favorite, Rudi Altig. The problem was that Anquetil and Poulidor disliked each other passionately. Each seemed to be more intent on ensuring the other didn't win than on chasing the prize for himself. With the help of others, Altig was able to make it back to the leaders. He attacked with a few hundred meters remaining while the two Frenchmen looked at each other. Neither would chase after Altig, for fear it would enable the other to win. Altig took the gold ahead of Anquetil and Poulidor.

There was further controversy after the race, when a number of riders refused to be tested by the UCI at the doping controls that had been introduced. Altig, Anquetil, Gianni Motta, Italo Zilioli, and Jean Stablinski refused to be tested, while Poulidor claimed to have gotten lost on his way to the doping control. They were initially suspended by the UCI, but subsequently cleared, and the result was allowed to stand.

At the 1974 World Championships, Freddy Maertens claimed that a laxative had been put in his drink during the race in Montreal. He said that it had been spiked by Eddy Merckx's soigneur, Gust Naessens, who had been handed the bottle while his own masseur, Jef D'Hont, had gone to get something to eat. Years afterward,

Maertens asked Naessens what had happened in Montreal; he is supposed to have replied, "It was normal, Freddy. I was asked to give you your drink and I put something in it. You were too good for my guy, so I put something in it to block you." It wouldn't be the only controversy involving the Belgian team.

The Belgian team worked well together in 2012 to help ensure victory, but national teams aren't always so cooperative in the World Championships.

In 1982 in Goodwood, the American cyclist Jonathan Boyer broke clear on his own. It seemed that he was on his way to victory—until who was to chase him down but his own teammate Greg Lemond. As soon as Boyer was caught, Italian Giuseppe Saronni made his move. He went on to win, while Lemond claimed the silver. When asked about his tactics years later, Lemond was unapologetic: "There was a lot said about that, and Boyer said I chased him down, but first of all we were not friends. The US team was not really a team that was together like they are today. We were really individuals in the same jersey. I wanted to win the world title. Now, you can say I might have had a better chance to if I'd let someone else do the chasing, but I didn't see it like that at the time." Lemond would go on to claim the title the following year.

Arguably the most controversial Worlds ever were those in Ronse (or Renaix if you're French speaking) in Belgium in 1988. That year, the local favorite Claude Criquielion and Canadian Steve Bauer clashed during the sprint finish, only to be overtaken by the Italian Maurizio Fondriest, who took the win. Criquielion and Fondriest were clear going into the last kilometer, but in the finishing straight Bauer joined them after a chase. Bauer opened the sprint from the left-hand side of the road, with the Belgian Criquielion on his right shoulder. They switched to the other side of the road, and with one hundred meters to go, it seemed that Fondriest was out of contention.

Criquielion tried to overtake his rival but hit his front wheel on the foot of one of the crowd barriers, and fell. The impact caused Bauer to lose momentum, enabling Fondriest to take the win. Bauer was later disqualified, and Criquielion decided to sue for assault. He filed a criminal lawsuit asking for $1.5 million in compensation. The case dragged on for five years, and was heard in three separate courts. The judges ruled in favor of Bauer each time. Bauer and Criquielion still don't speak, with the Canadian saying,

"I don't think I can ever forgive him for what he did. Nobody lets someone drag them through the courts for that long and then just says, 'Yeah, that was fun while it lasted and we are buddies now.' I don't think so."

Another unique aspect of the World Championships is that for one day of the cycling calendar, riders who are normally teammates are supposed to ride against each other. It doesn't always happen. At the 2005 World Championships in Madrid, two members of the British team, Charly Wegelius and Tom Southam, decided to ride in support of their trade teammates rather than their national team leader, Roger Hammond. This decision cost them dearly, as they wouldn't be selected for the Great British team again.

Down through the years, there have also been numerous rumors of money being offered between riders from different countries in exchange for assistance in winning the title. In 1962, Jean Stablinski was said to have offered money to two riders to help chase down the Irishman Shay Elliott. This was despite the fact that the two were friends.

Even the wearing of the rainbow jersey itself has sometimes caused trouble, with some team owners disliking the requirement for their rider to wear the shirt. The owner of the Festina team didn't look kindly on one of his team wearing the jersey. His directeur sportif, Bruno Roussel, said, "So, when I brought up the World Championship and its symbolic rainbow jersey, he was no more enthusiastic. 'I pay the riders all through the year to carry the name of my business,' he said, 'not to dress up like a paint factory.'"

What with squabbling teammates, unethical deals being done, and various other controversies, the race tends to be one of the highlights of the calendar. It's rarely predictable, and usually provides plenty of discussion points afterward, not least of which is whether the new winner will go on to struggle the following season.

2

The First Victim

The first cyclist whose name became synonymous with misfortune happening to a rainbow jersey winner was the Belgian Stan Ockers. This was despite the fact that the accident that happened to him took place shortly after his reign as World Champion was over.

Constant Ockers, or Stan as his family called him, was born in the suburbs of the port of Antwerp, and as a child had dreamed of joining the Belgian navy. He left school early with the intention of signing up, but, because of his young age, he had to initially content himself with becoming a painter in the shipyards. His career as a painter didn't last long, as his older brother Jos bought Stan a bike, and he quickly showed talent as a racing cyclist. However, he also loved soccer and was finding it difficult to balance the two sports. Eventually, cycling won out.

Ockers progressed through the amateur ranks quickly, and began his professional career in Nazi-occupied Belgium in 1941. In his first year, he had victories in criteriums in Sint-Niklaas, Stekene, and Schoten. He really showed his potential, though, with his victory in the Grote Scheldeprijs. His career progression was held up by external factors, however. The carnage of World War II had caused much disruption to the professional cycling calendar throughout Europe, so it was really in the postwar era that Ockers came to the fore. In 1947 at the age of twenty-seven, he came in second in the Tour of Switzerland, and three years later was second in the Tour de France.

He repeated this feat two years later, and in 1953 won La Flèche Wallonne for the first time. The diminutive Ockers (he was only five foot five) was a popular rider, but still had his detractors. He was called lazy by some riders, while others felt that he was a really good tactician and knew exactly when to make his efforts. That was the reason he was known to some as "the Mathematician." Cycling journalist Jos Van Landeghem was to say of him, "Stan wasn't the greatest talent of his generation, but he could read a race like no other. That was sometimes misinterpreted."

He divided opinion in the peloton, but the fans loved him. His popularity with cycling enthusiasts stemmed from the fact that he was seen as an everyman. He appealed to all social classes in Belgium, and was known for giving a lot of time to help young riders improve.

In 1955, Ockers was having his best year to date. He managed the difficult feat of winning the weekend Ardennais, as he captured both La Flèche Wallonne and Liège–Bastogne–Liège. At that time, the races were run on consecutive days, which makes the feat even more impressive. At Flèche, Ockers attacked before the Côte des Forges, and he increased his advantage further on the climb. He won alone by three minutes. At Liège the following day, he attacked with teammate Raymond Impanis. The duo stayed clear, with Ockers easily outsprinting his compatriot.

Ferdi Kübler was the only rider to have achieved this feat prior to Ockers. The Belgian could have also possibly won Paris–Roubaix that year, but didn't want to work against his Elvé-Peugeot team-mate Impanis.

Later that year, he went on to win the points classification in the Tour de France. Despite being thirty-five years old, it seemed that Ockers was getting stronger at an age when most cyclists had retired. Following the Tour, he set his sights on capturing the world title.

The World Championships that year was being held in Frascati, twenty kilometers southeast of Rome. Ockers had come close to victory in the past, having finished in third place in 1953 in Lugano behind Fausto Coppi and Germain Derijcke. Just five days prior to the race, Ockers had shown his continuing good form when he won his last preparation race prior to traveling to Italy, a kermesse in Bertrix in Belgium.

Among the other favorites lining up at the start were the new French star Jacques Anquetil and his compatriot Louison Bobet; the Italians Fausto Coppi and Gastone Nencini; and the Swiss rider Ferdi Kübler. It was an incredibly hot day, and it was predicted that it would be one of the most difficult World Championships in recent years.

The rivalry between Coppi and Bobet played into the Ockers's hands. They were marking each other so tightly that neither really had a chance that day. Halfway through the 293-kilometer race, it seemed that the race was also over for Ockers. A dangerous group had gone clear—containing Anquetil, Nencini, and André Darrigade, among others—and at one stage had gained a lead of over ten minutes on the peloton. The boisterous Italian crowd grew incensed at the lack of effort from the peloton in trying to bring the leaders back, and started booing the riders as they passed.

While Coppi and Louison Bobet watched each other and would eventually both retire from the race, Ockers went clear of the bunch, along with the Italian Bruno Monti and Pierre Molinéris of France. At least Monti's efforts gave the partisan crowd something to shout about. The trio gradually reduced the gap to the leaders, and on the penultimate lap they caught the front men. No sooner had they made it across than Ockers attacked on the climb. He quickly pulled clear alone as none of the others could hang on to his wheel. After nearly nine hours of cycling, he crossed the line solo to become the first Belgian World Champion since Briek Schotte in 1950. He finished more than a minute clear of Luxembourg's Jempy Schmitz and fellow Belgian Germain Derijcke. It was an indication of the difficulty of the race that Ferdi Kübler, who had won both the Tour de France and World Championships previously, came in nearly nineteen minutes behind. Only twenty of the sixty-five starters would finish the race.

Upon his return to Antwerp, crowds thronged the streets, causing trams to have to be diverted. Ockers was also asked to attend a reception in Brussels, where he was honored by King Baudouin. It was a reflection of the consistency he had shown that season that Ockers won the Challenge Desgrange-Colombo, as determined by his performances in the biggest races of the season.

Stan Ockers arrives home to Antwerp to a hero's welcome
after capturing the 1955 title.

Following his win in the Worlds, he was offered a lucrative contract for the following season with the Italian Girardengo team,
where he would team up with compatriot Rik Van Steenbergen, and
Spaniards Miguel Poblet and Federico Bahamontes.

Ockers started 1956 with great confidence. He came close to
taking another classic win when he finished second in the Tour of
Flanders and went one better when he won Roma–Napoli–Roma.
In the Tour de France, he repeated his performance of the year
before as he won the points classification, as well as winning the
stage to Saint-Étienne. He had done a great job in honoring the
rainbow jersey.

Unfortunately, Ockers was unable to retain his world title in

Copenhagen that year; his trade teammate Rik Van Steenbergen won the race. He made a respectable defense of his title, though, finishing outside the medal positions in fourth place.

Toward the end of September that year, Ockers was invited to take part in the Festival der Wegrenners at his home velodrome, the Sportpaleis in Antwerp. He had great experience riding on the track, and earlier that season had broken the world hour record behind a derny. This was to be his 116th appearance at the track. Competing alongside Ockers would be some of the other big stars of the sport, including Van Steenbergen, Rik Van Looy, and Fred De Bruyne, in addition to Charly Gaul, Roger Walkowiak, and Bernard Gauthier.

On the second night of the event, a break went clear in one of the events, and Ockers moved to the front of the group to try to bring them back. Ockers looked back to see who was on his wheel, but in doing so he didn't notice that one of the other riders, Nest Sterckx, had stopped on the track to check his wheel.

There was a massive collision as Ockers rode into Sterckx. Rik Van Looy and Gerrit Voorting were also involved, but Voorting and Sterckx were able to walk away. Van Looy and Ockers were more seriously hurt—both lay motionless on the track. They were taken away by stretcher to be seen by the Red Cross.

Van Looy regained consciousness after a few minutes. Ockers was initially diagnosed with a broken collarbone and concussion. However, it would turn out that his condition was much more serious than first suspected.

He was taken to nearby Saint Bartholomew's Hospital in Merksem, where the full extent of his injuries was realized the following morning. He had suffered a skull fracture; four ribs were also broken. Overnight he had drifted in and out of consciousness but eventually fell into a coma.

His situation deteriorated rapidly and later that day, he was given the last rites by a priest. Two trauma specialists arrived from Bruges and Brussels, and decided to bore into his skull to try to stop the hemorrhaging, but it was to no avail.

Two days after the accident, Ockers died of severe head injuries. An estimated ten thousand mourners attended his funeral. Among those who was said to have taken his death particularly badly was an eleven-year-old Eddy Merckx. Merckx would later say, "He was my hero when I was a young boy, but not because of the Classics. He was always in the news during the Tour de France, and the Tour de France was everything to me."

Ockers left behind a widow, Rosa, and six-year-old son, Eddy. A race was organized the following year in his memory. The first edition of the Grand Prix Stan Ockers was won appropriately enough by his friend Raymond Impanis, whom Stan had refused to chase down two years earlier in Paris–Roubaix. Unfortunately, the race named after him was discontinued after 1963.

Two memorials were later built to honor Ockers. One stands at the scene of his demise, the velodrome at Antwerp, while the other has been built at the summit of the Côte des Forges. The climb was chosen as it was where he had gone clear to win La Flèche-Wallonne, and it's still regularly used as part of the route of one of Ockers's other greatest triumphs, Liège–Bastogne–Liège. Ockers had joined the long list of riders who had crashed and died during a race, and in doing so became the first cyclist linked with the curse of the rainbow jersey.

3

The Treason of Ronse

Since the inaugural World Professional Championships in 1927, there had been just two riders who had won the title three times. After back-to-back wins in 1960 and 1961, it was felt by many that Rik Van Looy would join his compatriot Rik Van Steenbergen and Italian Alfredo Binda in becoming a member of this illustrious club.

Van Looy had emerged in the late 1950s as a tremendous talent in one-day races and would go on to win all of the Monuments. He was also a rider you didn't want to cross—he could make life very difficult for those who upset him. One of his weaknesses was incredible pride, and he took particular umbrage at one of the nicknames bestowed upon him. The Belgian press had started calling him Rik II (with Van Steenbergen now being referred to as Rik I), and the younger Belgian considered this somewhat patronizing. He much preferred his other nickname, the Emperor of Herentals.

The Belgian felt that the 1963 World Championships might offer him the best chance he would ever have of gaining his third win, as the event was taking place in Ronse in Belgium. The 279-kilometer race that year would turn out to be one of the most talked-about World Championship races ever, as Van Looy's predicted victory was stolen from him by one of his teammates. Cycling fans throughout Flanders would be divided in their opinions on the incident, and also dismayed by the stories that would later emerge of payments being made between riders.

Van Looy was considered one of the pre-race favorites, as in addition to his fearsome sprint he was also known for his tactical nous. A Belgian journalist at the time would describe Van Looy as "studying his opponents as a mongoose studies cobras, searching for signs of injuries that may slow them down or force them to change their regular pattern of racing. He memorizes every course, locating trouble spots where accidents or traffic jams are likely to occur, picking his spots for passing and for his final sprint."

By his own high standards, Van Looy had not had the best of seasons, but he'd still taken the Belgian title and the green jersey in the Tour de France. Even though he had only a handful of wins coming into the World Championships, he still demanded that the whole team ride in support of him. The Belgian federation also backed him up, and demanded that every team member sign a contract to this effect. Emile Daems argued that all team members should be given an opportunity—and he had, after all, won both Milan–San Remo and Paris–Roubaix previously. Daems was thanked by the federation for being so open and honest, and promptly dropped from the team.

The selection of the team would be based on who would ride for Rik II, and the manager of the Groene Leeuw team, Albert de Kimpe, pushed for the inclusion of his protégé Benoni Beheyt, indicating that the young man would prove to be a valuable domestique. Beheyt was still only twenty-two, and had shown great promise by winning Ghent–Wevelgem and the Tour de Wallonie earlier in the season.

Each member of the team was promised ten thousand Belgian francs if he helped Van Looy win the race, and Beheyt didn't hesitate to accept. It was a great opportunity to earn some decent money. Van Looy must have also considered that less experienced team members like Beheyt would be less likely to go against team orders. How wrong he was.

The circuit in Ronse was fairly flat albeit with some cobbled sections, and the Belgian team did a great job in controlling the race for the first few laps. Beheyt demonstrated his loyalty to his team leader early on when he chased after Raymond Poulidor. After he caught the Frenchman, he refused to contribute to the escape. Other Belgian team members Pino Cerami and Gilbert Desmet chased down breaks by Tom Simpson of Great Britain and the Dutchman Jo de Haan, respectively.

It seemed to be all going to plan for Van Looy, but three laps from the end, two danger men escaped. Simpson attacked again, with the Irishman Shay Elliott. Elliott was noncommittal about the break, and Simpson tried to persuade him to work more. Simpson would later reveal that he tried to pay the Irishman to work, saying, "I offered him the same price that van Looy was giving his team but he told me it wasn't enough. I doubled it in desperation, as I really did so want to win and especially to beat the Belgian combine."

It's unclear whether Elliott had also been offered money by Van Looy, as it was not unknown for money to exchange hands between rival team members. Alternatively, the Irishman may have been reluctant to work against some of his trade teammates, such as Jacques Anquetil. Regardless, Simpson's efforts came to nothing.

Coming into the last lap, the much-reduced peloton was all together, and it was looking good for Van Looy. However, Gilbert Desmet saw his own chance on the run in to the finish and attacked against team orders. The speed within the group was so high that Desmet stood no chance. It was getting tense, with a lot of jostling for position. Simpson was still hanging on in the group, and recalled afterward, "I would not have won, as there were a number of much better sprinters around me but then, bang! Van Looy grabbed me by the jersey and just about brought me to a standstill!" That was only the start of it. No sooner had Simpson regained his momentum than Jan Janssens was hanging off his jersey.

With only a few kilometers remaining, the work done by the Belgians had taken its toll, and there was nobody left to help Van Looy get himself into a good position for the sprint. Coming under the red kite signifying the last kilometer of the race, he looked for a teammate to lead him out, and saw Beheyt. However, the younger man claimed he had cramps and couldn't help. Van Looy would have to do it himself. Simpson made another attempt to go clear, but was brought back by Desmet.

Despite the group being down to just twenty-eight riders, it still contained some danger men, with sprinters of the caliber of André

Darrigade still present. It may have been a combination of the presence of these threats and the lack of support that caused Van Looy to panic and open up his sprint on the right-hand side of the road with four hundred meters remaining. With two hundred meters to go, Van Looy hit the front. It was looking good for the Emperor.

Van Looy then saw a threat moving up on the other side of the road. It was Beheyt. Instinctively, Van Looy moved across to try to block off the challenge. Beheyt feared that he would be knocked off his bike, and reached out to grab his teammate's jersey. It appeared to some that not only did he hold on to Van Looy's jersey to keep himself upright, but he also pulled him back. In doing so, Van Looy lost his momentum, and Beheyt crossed the line first. Immediately upon crossing the line, Van Looy started gesticulating with his teammate.

Tom Simpson, who had himself been tugged by Van Looy in the sprint, recalled, "Van Looy was shouting desperately for someone to give him a wheel to pace him to the front. He asked Benoni Beheyt but was told he had cramp. Beheyt was foxing and, taking the inside, had gone to the front under his own power. As I was told, van Looy saw him and switched across the road trying to ward him off. Just about side by side, Beheyt got hold of van Looy's jersey and I reckon he must have said to himself, 'Should I push him? Should I hell!' And so he pulled him as his captain was trying to push him away, and he took the title by inches."

Looking at the grainy video footage of the race, it is difficult to determine exactly what happened. It appears that Beheyt was fending Van Looy off to avoid a crash, but whether he actually pulled him back by the jersey is another matter.

As Beheyt was being hoisted upon the shoulders of his supporters, Van Looy was livid, and was filing a complaint with the race jury. This complaint was rejected. In fact, Van Looy was informed that he was closer to being disqualified than Beheyt. The jury may have backed down from overturning the result, as disqualifying the Belgian duo would have resulted in the unthinkable situation of the Dutchman Jo de Haan winning on Belgian soil.

Benoni Beheyt fends off his teammate Rik Van Looy to cross the line first.

At the medal ceremony, Beheyt was jeered by many in the crowd as the rainbow jersey was placed on him. The disgust was etched on Van Looy's face. Supporters of Beheyt would claim that their man saw Van Looy starting to fade, and that he only overtook him to ensure Belgium claimed the title. Beheyt himself stated that he had simply eased himself past Van Looy and held out his hand to prevent them from bumping into each other.

Beheyt was shocked by the reaction of the crowd. "People began to shout at me," he said. "I didn't know what I had done. I was the strongest that day." One Belgian journalist would later describe him melodramatically as "a swindler, a knight of barbaric origin."

One man who did take particular pleasure in the result was Beheyt's trade team manager, Albert de Kimpe. Not only did he now have a World Champion on his team, but he had also placed a hefty wager on his rider prior to the race. He must have known that Beheyt had no intention of following team orders.

Van Looy recalled the incident: "When I think about it now, what I did was not in my character. Simpson broke away in the last kilometer. Desmet jumped after him, but I thought he would not be able to bridge the gap. Hence, I jumped too, but I caught Simpson too quickly, about two or three hundred meters from the line. I was in my big ring and couldn't continue the effort. I wanted to, but my legs said 'no, no, that's too much.'

"Then I happened to see Beheyt there and I asked myself 'What's he doing there? We had an agreement, didn't we?' This was the reason I swerved, to crowd him a little. But he had passed me and his reaching out to push me back was completely normal. It was his right because I had shut the door on him. I went to the podium that time," he concluded, laughing. (This was a reference to the 1957

World Championships where Van Looy had not attended the medal ceremony, as he thought only the winner had to.)

Years later, Van Looy would elaborate further, and seemed to contradict his earlier recollections. "It was a pull," he said. "And there's another thing, if I'd known Beheyt was going to sprint, I would have done my sprint differently. In the finale, Beheyt told me he had cramp, and wouldn't be able to do anything."

The following year, Beheyt made a great attempt to honor the rainbow jersey: He came in second in the Tour of Flanders, won a stage of the Tour de France, and also won the Tour of Belgium overall. However, Beheyt did not have many friends in the peloton after Ronse for two reasons: He had reneged on the pre-race agreement to help Van Looy, and had brought a lot of bad publicity to the sport. There were numerous articles about race fixing and selling of races following his victory. Also, Van Looy let it be known that he would not look favorably upon anyone—riders or race promoters— who aided Beheyt's career. Tom Simpson reckoned that if you weren't a friend of the Emperor, you wouldn't make any money in Belgium.

Beheyt did initially get a lot of publicity out of the incident, and made some good money from criteriums. However, he wouldn't win anything of note after 1964. Van Looy was diplomatic (in public, at least) about the incident, but Beheyt's career was effectively over. He would ride the Tour de France twice more after his World Championship win, but only because the race was once again open to sponsored trade teams rather than national teams. Because Beheyt was a member of the Wiel's Groene Leeuw team and Van Looy was with Solo-Superia, the older man was in no position to keep him from the race.

He continued on as a professional until 1968, when he retired at the age of twenty-seven, with nineteen victories to his name. The trouble arising from his World Championship win was the main reason for his early retirement, but others blamed a lack of ambition, poor discipline, and family problems. A doping affair in 1965 would not have helped, either. Beheyt himself was initially vague when asked what prompted his retirement, saying, "I didn't have much desire for racing."

Years later, however, he would reveal a little more. "In 1965, I got married. I became tired of driving everywhere, and I didn't have much enthusiasm for racing anymore. In 1966, I took over the running of my parents' bike shop."

Van Looy would continue winning races until his retirement in 1970, but he didn't win that elusive third world title. Beheyt still appears at races, but doesn't feel comfortable talking about the incident in 1963. His grandson Guillaume Van Keirsbulck would also go on to become a professional cyclist. Beheyt and Van Looy have since put the dispute behind them, and in 2004 they helped to carry the coffin of another Belgian World Champion, Briek Schotte.

The other pallbearers included Eddy Merckx, Roger De Vlaeminck, and Freddy Maertens, who would also have disagreements among themselves during their careers. When Merckx had arrived on the scene, the Emperor did not appreciate being upstaged by the new kid on the block. It was said that he had ensured that Merckx had no chance of winning the 1969 World Championships when he realized that he could not win himself.

It was a reflection of the strength of Belgian cycling at the time that it seemed there were too many great cyclists trying to share the top races. Inevitably there would be clashes, and the disagreement between Beheyt and Van Looy was one of the nastiest. Years later, when Beheyt was asked by a Belgian journalist whether he believed in the curse of the rainbow jersey, he responded with a curt, "Those are myths."

4

Mr. Tom

Drugs have been linked with cycling since the advent of the sport in the late 1800s, with Welshman Arthur Linton being one of the first reported cyclists to die from drug use. Linton had been taking part in Bordeaux–Paris in 1896, and died a few weeks after competing. It was said that his death was caused by a combination of drug-induced exhaustion and typhoid fever. Many others have died since then, but the name that became most synonymous with the problem of drugs in the sport was Tom Simpson.

The Englishman collapsed and died on the slopes of Mont Ventoux during the 1967 Tour de France. It later emerged that amphetamines had been found in his back pocket. Everybody who knew Simpson felt that he was willing to push himself harder than others, and that he was willing to do whatever was needed to win the Tour de France. As early as 1960, Simpson had discussed the temptations of doping in an interview with the English newspaper *The Observer*.

He was to say, "I am up there with the stars, but then suddenly they will get away from me. I know from the way they ride that they are taking dope. I don't want to have to take it—I have too much respect for my body, but if I don't win a big event soon, I shall have to start taking it."

Simpson was one of the emerging English-speaking pioneers who were establishing themselves as genuine contenders on the Continent. He had been developing a decent palmarès, and prior to the '65 season had won the Tour of Flanders, Bordeaux–Paris, and Milan–San Remo. Among the other races that he craved victory in was the World Championships.

Simpson's preparation for the 1965 World Championships had received a serious setback in the Tour de France. He had developed an abscess in the palm of his hand, which caused him to abandon the race. The resulting operation kept him off the bike for ten days. Although he was massively disappointed at the time, in some ways this affliction possibly helped him: Thanks to his low profile, he was no longer considered one of the favorites. He was also well rested.

He had come close to winning the Worlds before. Two years earlier when Benoni Beheyt had won, he had been caught within a few hundred meters of the finish line. The following year, Simpson had come close to a podium position, finishing in fourth place, just six seconds behind the winner, Dutchman Jan Janssens. It seemed that he was destined to win the title some year.

The race was being held in the Basque country that year, and Simpson felt super confident of a good ride. He had traveled down with the Australian rider Nev Veale and revealed his self-belief to his traveling companion. Simpson said that he was so sure that he would win, he even started planning what he would do to celebrate. In the days preceding the race, he trained with the rest of the British team on the circuit, and the other team members could see that he was looking very fit.

Ninety-six riders lined up at the start in Lasarte, ten kilometers south of San Sebastián, where they would have to face fourteen laps of a nineteen-kilometer circuit in torrential rain. An early break went clear at the end of the first lap, which Simpson missed. It was quite a dangerous group as it contained Dutchman Peter Post and the Italian Franco Balmamion, among others. Simpson sensed the danger and managed to bridge across to the leaders on the third lap, along with the German Rudi Altig. The break worked well together, and by the halfway point they were three minutes clear of the chasers. This lead group contained five Spanish riders, so the locals were ecstatic.

Simpson revealed later that he felt Altig and Post were the danger men he would need to look out for—but there were still too many riders in the group, and it would need to be whittled down. With two laps remaining, the Englishman attacked on the main climb of the circuit in his biggest gear. Only Altig was able to stick with him. The two had shown previously that they could work well together: They had been partners in the Baracchi Trophy, a two-man time trial the previous year, and had finished in third place.

On the second-to-the-last climb of Hernani, Altig asked Simpson to slow down and unknowingly gave his breakaway partner a psychological advantage. He knew then that Altig was struggling and he could beat him. The two were still clear on the last lap, and came to an agreement: Coming into the last kilometer, each would take one side of the road, so that neither had to lead out the sprint. The race would be decided by who had the strongest sprint that day, rather than through tactics. Simpson recounted the last few kilometers in his autobiography *Cycling Is My Life*.

"I led all the way down that final descent and through the packed, cheering streets of Lasarte. As we approached the kilometer sign we dutifully parted and came towards the line side by side. I started my sprint a few hundred yards out and kept going as hard as I could. I didn't look ahead at all. I was looking down, looking for his shadow on the road as he came up on me. I kept thinking, 'he's coming, he's coming, he's coming.' And suddenly, when I was ten yards from the line it dawned on me. 'He hasn't, he hasn't made it. It's mine,' and I was over the line, grinning like a maniac, heart pounding and tears welling up in my eyes."

It was claimed afterward that Altig had tried to buy the win from Simpson but was turned down. The German had supposedly asked him, "How much would it take for you to lose this title, Tom?" Simpson said that when he was asked that, he knew the title was his.

It could have turned out very differently however, as he realized after he had crossed the finish line. He looked at his bike and noticed a problem. "As I looked at the tires I found that the rear one had a two-inch strip worn away," he said, "with strands of rubber hanging free, it was bulging at the side and was on the point of bursting at any moment."

The night of his win, Simpson couldn't believe what he had

achieved and he had a somewhat restless sleep, getting up a number of times throughout the night to look at himself in the mirror with his rainbow jersey on. He was sharing a room with the Frenchman Jean Stablinski that night, who eventually told him to just keep it on and go back to sleep.

His reign in the rainbow colors could not have gotten off to a better start. Having already taken victories in Milan–San Remo and the Tour of Flanders, a month after the World Championships he notched up his third win in one of the great one-day classics, the Tour of Lombardy. He had become only the second reigning World Champion to win in Lombardy—and you had to look as far back as Alfredo Binda to find the first to achieve this feat, in 1927.

At the age of twenty-seven, Simpson had now won three out of the five classics that were considered Monuments. There was every possibility that he could go on to win both Paris–Roubaix and Liège–Bastogne–Liège at some stage during the rest of his career. At that time, Rik Van Looy was the only rider to have achieved that feat. However, it was not to be, and Lombardy would turn out to be his last big win in a one-day race.

At the end of the season, he achieved another first. Up until then, no cyclist had won the prestigious BBC Sports Personality of the Year, but Simpson was awarded the trophy that year. He was in much demand that winter and revealed to friends that he expected the win to bring him more than thirty-six thousand pounds in earnings over the coming year.

Despite his busy schedule, he still managed to find time to relax.

In the off-season, cyclists tried to find other ways to maintain their fitness, and an option chosen by many was downhill skiing. Jacques Anquetil had a house in Saint-Gervais, which became the base for a lot of cyclists to try their hand at the sport. The Italian aperitif producer Martini even sponsored an annual race there, contested by both professional cyclists and journalists. Simpson was one of those who made the trip there the winter after his triumph at the Worlds, along with Ferdinand Bracke and Jan Janssens.

Unfortunately, he had a fall on the slopes and was hurt pretty badly. Coincidentally, his accident was on the same day, January 25, as another skiing accident the previous year, but this one was more serious. Simpson broke his right tibia, and had to have his whole leg encased in plaster. The cast would stay on until the end of February.

In the short term, Simpson had to miss out on some lucrative contracts for track appearances at Antwerp and Milan. He said in his autobiography, "Since I started on this book I have broken a leg, having had a couple of skiing accidents on exactly the same day in successive years. This makes me wonder if bad luck is dogging me still but I am not moaning."

Years afterward, his fellow British professional Michael Wright would be less forgiving in his opinion of the accident. "Sometimes [Simpson] didn't think," he said. "The ski accident came just when he could have started to make serious money, but the start of that season was ruined."

Simpson traveled to see his agent, Daniel Dousset, to come up

L'Equipe/Offside

Tom Simpson with Rudi Altig, the man he outsprinted to take the world title. His reign in the rainbow jersey was hampered by injury.

with a plan for salvaging the rest of his season. Dousset was supposed to have been less than pleased, to put it mildly. Simpson's widow, Helen, would recall his reaction. "Dousset liked flamboyant, extrovert guys because he could market them. There were times though when Tom would rub him up the wrong way. Tom went skiing when he was World Champion, broke his leg and Dousset went off his rocker."

Dousset—who had been compared by one commentator to a Mafia hit man—was livid with the Englishman, as he earned 10 percent of the rider's earnings. However, Simpson had some good news for his agent and team manager: Doctors told him that the injury was healing well, and that he would back racing in March. When his cast did eventually get removed, his left leg had lost a considerable amount of muscle mass; he found it difficult even to get out of the saddle. Yet he was still able to start his first race two weeks later.

He did go on to win a number of small criteriums that spring in France, but he had no results of note. His main aim of the season was the Tour de France, and he still felt he had time to recover his form before *La Grand Boucle*. However, his attempts there did not exactly go to plan. He came close to a stage victory, finishing second on two stages, but was to crash out of the race after falling on the descent of the Col du Galibier.

Following the Tour, Simpson won some more criteriums, but he went through the entire season without capturing any major races. He made an appearance at the World Championships in Nürburgring, but he was never really in contention. At the end of the year, Simpson and his family forwent a skiing holiday and instead traveled to Corsica, where they would engage in safer activities. He was now twenty-nine years of age, and he knew he would only have a few more seasons in which to earn enough to provide a comfortable life for his wife and young family.

That year, Simpson made the conscious decision to aim to win the Tour de France, and to prepare by riding more stage races rather than concentrating on the spring classics. He had a promising result for his Tour ambitions early on that year, as he won Paris–Nice. It seemed now that he had a different view on the topic of doping from earlier in his career. In an article for *The People* newspaper, he alluded to the fact that he was taking substances: "I honestly don't think much doping, in the worst sense of the word, goes on in cycling. Tell me where you draw the line between dope and tonics. Even the experts don't agree on that one."

The Tour started off well for Simpson, who was lying in sixth place after the first week. He had finished in seventh place on the stage to Roubaix, and then fifth on the stage that ended on Ballon d'Alsace. It looked like he might be one of the favorites for the overall win, which would be an open race given the non-appearance of Jacques Anquetil. However, Simpson began to slip down on General Classification, as he was affected by a stomach bug.

On the tenth stage, he lost a considerable amount of time to race leader and his trade teammate Roger Pingeon, and was now over eight minutes behind. One of the best opportunities that he would have to regain any time on the Frenchman would be on the 211-kilometer thirteenth stage from Marseilles to Carpentras.

That morning as the riders assembled for the start in Marseilles, the temperature was already creeping into the eighties. They were expected to reach the main difficulty of the day, and one of the most feared climbs in France, Mont Ventoux in the afternoon, when the temperature would be at its highest.

The climb hadn't been used in over a decade following the incidents in the 1955 Tour. That year, the French rider Jean Malléjac had lost consciousness and collapsed on the Ventoux, and had to be resuscitated by Dr. Pierre Dumas. Journalist Jacques Augendre described the scene in *L'Équipe*: "Pouring with sweat, haggard and semi-comatose, he zigzagged on a road which was no longer wide enough for him. He was no longer in the material world, still less that of cycling and the Tour de France."

In the ambulance on the way down the mountain, Malléjac was delirious, and Augendre said that he "talked, waved his arms, yelled, asked the way to the finish, and wanted to be let out." He wasn't the only rider to suffer on the mountain that day, as others collapsed and required oxygen. Since then, the organizers had been very reluctant to use the climb in the Tour.

When the race set off from Marseilles, there was much apprehension within the peloton about what lay ahead of them. The Tour's doctor, Pierre Dumas, had that morning prophetically said that, "if the riders take something today, we'll have a death on our hands." Race organizers limited the number of bottles that riders could take, and they were often seen to grab what they could from roadside bars. Simpson seemed to be suffering early on in the stage, and was seen drinking brandy. The alcohol would prove to be one of the fatal ingredients in his dehydration.

The slopes of Mont Ventoux become very exposed after Chalet Reynard, and there is no hiding place from the sun. With about three kilometers remaining in the climb, the Englishman collapsed. His manager ran to his aid, and he managed to cycle on a little farther before collapsing for the final time. Dr. Dumas was quickly on the scene. He understood the urgency of the situation and ordered a helicopter to airlift Simpson to the nearest hospital in Avignon.

The postmortem later showed that he had taken amphetamines and alcohol, which contributed to his death. The autopsy report stated: "Death was due to cardiac collapse which may be put down to exhaustion, in which unfavorable weather conditions, an excessive workload, and the use of medicines of the type discovered on the victim may have played a part. The dose of amphetamine ingested by Simpson should not have led to his death on its own, but on the other hand it could have led him to go beyond the limit of his strength and thus bring on the appearance of certain troubles linked to his exhaustion."

There was some discussion among the teams and organizers as to what to do next. Canceling the race was one suggestion. Finally, the decision was made to continue but to neutralize the following day's stage from Carpentras to Sète. Simpson's teammate Barry Hoban crossed the line first, which caused controversy with another member of the British team, Simpson's friend Vin Denson.

His funeral was held in Harworth in Nottinghamshire where his family had moved after the war. It was attended by Eddy Merckx, among others, whom he had raced with on the Peugeot team.

Afterward, some commentators made the direct link between Simpson's skiing accident at the start of the 1966 season and his death on Mont Ventoux. After his difficult 1966 season, it was said that his manager, Daniel Dousset, had warned him that he needed a great performance in the 1967 Tour or his career was as good as over.

However, Simpson's nephew, Chris Sidwells, would later say in his biography of his uncle, *Mr. Tom*, "I don't believe that the crash damaged him financially as much as some rumors that have sprung up since his death would have it. It was certainly not the reason why he was desperate to win the 1967 Tour de France, nor why he would go to any lengths to win it."

The year afterward, the Tour was billed as the "Tour of Health," and the organizers made a number of changes. Riders were now allowed to take water bottles from their team cars, and rest days were reintroduced. There were an increased number of drugs tests, with Jean Stablinski being kicked off the race after failing one. Despite these measures, however, the Tour would continue to be beset by drug scandals in the following decades. Simpson's death should have marked a turning point in the fight against drugs in the sport, but unfortunately didn't.

A memorial was built on the slopes of Mont Ventoux at the point where Simpson collapsed, and it has become a place of pilgrimage for cyclists in the decades since his death. Numerous other professional cyclists have died in the intervening years due to the use of drugs, but Simpson's death is possibly the most widely cited as the example of what can happen when cyclists push themselves too far in the pursuit of glory.

5

The Eagle of Hoogerheide

In 1969, the world of cycling was dominated by the young Belgian rider Eddy Merckx. That year alone, he had already racked up victories in Paris–Nice, Milan–San Remo, the Tour of Flanders, Liège–Bastogne–Liège, and the Tour de France, among many other wins. By the time the World Championships were due to take place, many riders appeared to be more interested in stopping Merckx from winning than in trying to chase for victory themselves. One cyclist in particular who did not take too kindly to being upstaged by his younger compatriot was Rik Van Looy. "Emperor Rik" was at the tail end of an amazing career in which he had won all of the one-day Monuments of the sport. However, he was now thirty-five years of age and had very limited success that season. In fact, it didn't even look like he was going to be selected for the Belgian team, until he won a stage of the Tour de France.

The Dutch team aimed to take advantage of the infighting among the Belgians, and in Jan Janssens they had one of the favorites for the race. The bespectacled Janssens had won the Worlds in 1964, and had also won the previous year's Tour de France. Unfortunately for Janssens, he was taken ill a week prior to the Worlds and had to withdraw from the team. The governing body for Dutch cycling, the KNWU, convened to decide on a replacement, and after much discussion decided to select little-known rider Harmin Ottenbros, more commonly known as Harm. Up until that point, Ottenbros's successes had been limited to a couple of stage wins in the Tour of Switzerland and some small kermesses. This decision to select Ottenbros would change the course not only of his cycling career but also his life.

The World Championships were being held that year at the Zolder motor racing circuit. The circuit would host the Belgian Grand Prix on ten occasions, but probably became best known as the place where the Canadian Formula One driver Gilles Villeneuve was killed during qualifying at the 1982 Belgian Grand Prix.

It was baking hot, even in the morning, as the peloton set off at the start of the 263-kilometer race. The temperature would reach nearly 104 degrees later that day. A dangerous break went clear early on in the race, which included Walter Godefroot, Michele Dancelli, and Julien Stevens. They would be joined afterward by another group that included Roger De Vlaeminck, Gerben Karstens, and Harm Ottenbros. Merckx also tried to bridge across, but every time he jumped clear he was chased down by Van Looy and the Italian Marino Basso, among others. It was evident to Van Looy that he was unable to win the race, but this didn't stop him from preventing his younger teammate from winning.

As the cat-and-mouse tactics continued in the bunch, the break worked well together; their lead grew as the laps progressed. The two strongest riders in the break were De Vlaeminck and Karstens. However, each time one of them would try to break clear, the other would drag the rest of the break back to them.

By this time, Merckx had grown weary of being chased down continuously and, realizing he would not win, decided to abandon. Many of the 150,000 spectators jeered Merckx as he climbed off his bike. His teammate Julien Stevens—also a trade teammate of Merckx's—upon hearing that he no longer had a team leader to work for, took his opportunity with both hands. After an attack by Dancelli was brought back with thirty kilometers remaining, Stevens counterattacked, and the only man who could hang on was Otten-bros. The pair worked well together and started to pull clear of the remainder of the break. Of the two, Stevens was clearly the favorite, as he had won a stage of the Tour de France earlier that summer, and was also a previous Belgian champion.

Their lead grew, and it was clear as they started the final lap that the pair would stay clear. During the final ascent of the Bolderberg, Stevens tried to drop his fellow escapee, but he couldn't shake the Dutchman. The race would be decided by a sprint between the two.

Coming into the final kilometer, the pair almost came to a stand-still as each tried to get the other to lead out the sprint. In the end, they were equally astute, and it came down to a straight sprint. They opened up with less than three hundred meters to go. Stevens's acceleration was quicker and he drew a couple of meters clear of his breakaway companion. However, as the finish line neared, Ottenbros started to close the gap. The Dutchman made a desperate lunge as they crossed the line, and the spectators could not make the call as to who won. After a few minutes' hesitation, the judges announced that Ottenbros was the victor, by a few centimeters.

"It was an odd feeling," Ottenbros would recount years later. "The nearer the finish line came, the more I had to tell myself I was just in a kermesse, although with a few more spectators than usual. I had to forget that I was riding for a world title because if I'd realized that, I'd never have won."

Dancelli jumped clear of the remainder of the break to take the bronze medal; Van Looy could only manage twenty-fourth place. Stevens was despondent as he knew this might be the best opportunity he ever had to become the World Champion. The Belgian gave his opinion to reporters afterward.

"I felt strong. Too strong, that's what I know now. In the final straight line we almost made a tactical standstill, Ottenbros took over, but it was I who launched the sprint and that's where I probably lost the victory. For the final 50 meters were slightly downhill and there was no wind. Ottenbros was perfectly launched."

The fallout from Ottenbros's victory was almost immediate. Journalists did not feel that he was a worthy victor, and was just lucky. Pierre Chany writing in *L'Équipe* said, "This World Championship, just as we'd forecast, was held to ransom right from the start by the formula of national teams, by disagreements among the Belgians, and by the aim of the peloton, which was to stop Eddy Merckx winning. The race needed a winner, and it was Ottenbros: Ottenbros, who finished the Tour de France in 78th place, three hours behind the yellow jersey. He was escorted to the podium by just his team manager and two policemen." Chany was inferring that the Dutchman had few supporters that day.

Other journalists were even more forthright, claiming that Ottenbros had no right to be the winner. Nor was it just journalists who displayed their vitriol. Race organizers, fans, and even riders made no attempt to hide their displeasure in seeing the young Dutchman take the title.

In fact, one of the only riders who offered his congratulations to Ottenbros was the Italian Franco Bitossi. Bitossi rode up alongside him in the Tour of Flanders the following spring and told him that he admired what he had done. So grateful was Ottenbros for the words of encouragement from the Italian that he would later give Bitossi one of his rainbow jerseys.

Ottenbros had already had problems at the start of the 1970 season, when he rode into a ravine in the Ruta del Sol and tore his calf muscle. He suffered more misfortune in the Tour of Flanders, when he fell and broke his wrist. It was a complicated break that would scupper much of his season. Just as he started to recover from his wrist injury, he became ill with intestinal problems, and he would not be able to defend his title at the World Championships, being held in England. Toward the end of the season, he received the news that his team sponsor, Willem II, a manufacturer of cigars, was to cease backing the team due to restrictions on the advertisement of tobacco. It had been a disastrous year for Ottenbros, who had only one victory to his name, a stage of the Tour of Luxembourg. He was not sorry to see his stint in the rainbow jersey come to an end.

Harm Ottenbros endured a very difficult year in the rainbow jersey.

"Believe me," he said afterward, "I wasn't in the slightest bit sorry when my year was as World Champion over and I didn't have to wear that jersey any more. I could just go back to being the unknown rider in village criteriums."

However, relinquishing the rainbow jersey did not solve Ottenbros's problems. He managed to get a contract with the Gazelle

team, but the money on offer was considerably less than what an
ex–World Champion should expect. Big wins continued to elude
him, and his form went from bad to worse. He was often seen struggling on even the smallest hills, and now insult was added to injury
as riders now started to call him "the Eagle of Hoogerheide." This
was a mocking reference to the great Spanish climber Federico Bahamontes, who was known as "the Eagle of Toledo," and also to the
fact that his home town of Hoogerheide was pancake-flat. "That
nickname made me more famous than my World Championship
ever did," Ottenbros told *L'Équipe*.

When asked whether he felt that he was a lucky winner that day,
he replied, "I was the strongest rider on the day. Or do you reckon
that I bribed all the other 190 riders? Don't forget that they all
wanted to be World Champion as well. I raced and they didn't. I
can't be held to blame if the stars of the day didn't take their chance."
Nobody could question the strength of the field that he had beaten
that day. Apart from the aforementioned Merckx, Godefroot, and
De Vlaeminck, he had also had to compete against Jacques Anquetil,
Rudi Altig, and Raymond Poulidor.

Ottenbros struggled to obtain any contracts for the lucrative criterium circuit, and even when he did he would struggle to get paid
by the organizers. The stress and misfortune played havoc with his
personal life also. As his career petered out, Ottenbros became ever
more depressed, to the point that he was contemplating suicide. He
had had enough of the bike. Finally in 1976, along with Gerrie
Knetemann, he cycled to the Oosterschelde storm surge barrier in

Zeeland and launched his bike into the sea. He had wanted to make a big statement showing that he was no longer interested cycling. He got a lift back on Knetemann's crossbar. Ottenbros admitted many years later, "I stayed cycling until 1976 because for a while it was my livelihood. But when I stopped, it was a relief."

It seemed that his life had hit rock bottom, but unfortunately things were to get worse. His marriage broke up, and he lost touch with his three children. Without anywhere else to live, he moved into a squat in Dordrecht in the province of South Holland and slept on the floor for two years, surrounded by other homeless people. He grew a beard and stopped cutting his hair. Within a short time, he was unrecognizable as the fit athlete he had been just a few years previously.

"I had money in the bank," he said, "but I never touched it. I wanted nothing to do with cycling and the self-centered life that had led to my divorce. As a cyclist you live in an imaginary world, you feel superior to everyone and everything, but that greatness is based on nothing."

Ottenbros tried to forget about the bike. His friend and former cyclist Eef Dolman found him a job, albeit voluntary, working in nearby Sliedrecht with children with intellectual disabilities. He gained an interest in sculpture, but gave up when he feared that people might recognize his name, and he would become the subject of ridicule again.

In the intervening years, Ottenbros has rebuilt his life. He now lives in rented accommodations just south of Rotterdam. He has regained his confidence, and after shunning the limelight and the cycling world for many years, he has started to reappear at bike races.

The supervisor at the clinic where Ottenbros had volunteered was really impressed with his work ethic and offered him a full-time position; he still works helping children with difficulties. He has also taken up sculpting again and has even rejoined his old cycling club, Alkmaar Victrix. He still has his rainbow jersey and medal in a cupboard. But it's been years since he looked at them.

The Eagle of Hoogerheide admits that he made mistakes in his early years as a professional, living a life of excess, but he has become a lot more philosophical in the intervening period. He forgets much of what happened in his darkest years and admits that he doesn't really want to remember that time.

He is healthy once again and content with his life, but still harbors one regret: "If I could live my life all over again, I'd miss out the cycling bit."

6

Jempi

Of all the bad luck that has befallen wearers of the rainbow jersey, there is possibly none as tragic as that of the Belgian cyclist Jean-Pierre Monseré. He was only twenty-one years old when he won his title, but within a matter of months tragedy would strike the man who had been considered to be one of the most prodigious talents seen in the sport in recent decades.

Although his father, Achilles, had been a cyclist himself, he persuaded his only son, born on September 8, 1948, in Roeselare in West Flanders, to take up football. Jean-Pierre showed great talent as a goalkeeper until he suffered a severe concussion from an accident on the pitch. He gave up the sport soon afterward and asked his father to buy him a bicycle, which Achilles agreed to, so long as his school grades were good.

From the start, Jean-Pierre was winning races, taking 115 victories as a juvenile. As he progressed through the amateur ranks, he decided that he was going to try to make it as a professional. His parents fully supported his decision. Jean-Pierre, or "Jempi" as he was nicknamed, was selected for the 1968 Olympics, where he finished sixth in the road race.

Around this time, Jempi met a local girl, Annie Victor, at a dance hall in Izegem. She was three years younger than him, and she can still vividly recall their first meeting. "He told me, 'If I win next week, the flowers are for you.' And indeed, the next time we met, he gave me flowers. I thought he was such a nice guy." They would marry quite soon afterward, and move in with his parents.

The following year, Jempi did even better when he finished second in the Amateur World Championships, in Brno in the Czech Republic, behind the Dane Leif Mortensen. Immediately after the championships, on September 4, he signed a professional contract with the Flandria team. One of his first races was the Italian semi-classic Coppa Agostoni, where he surprised many by finishing second behind Franco Bitossi.

The following week, in the Giro di Lombardia, Jempi did even better. He made it into the front group of nine who were to fight out the finish in the Stadio Giuseppe Sinigaglia. Franco Bitossi led out a long sprint but was overtaken by the Dutchman Gerben Karstens. Jempi managed to get second. A few days afterward, however, Karstens tested positive for drugs and the victory was handed to Monseré. It was a phenomenal win for a neophyte professional.

Jean-Pierre and Annie had even more reason to celebrate that year, as their son Giovanni was born. Annie recalled that "Jean-Pierre was almost crazy when Giovanni was born. A boy was a dream come true. They looked very similar, with the same coloring and the same eyes."

The 1970 season augured well for Jean-Pierre, but he didn't start out as well as he had hoped. He had won a couple of stages in the

Ruta del Sol in the early part of the season, but not a lot else. Jempi didn't have many opportunities as the year progressed to add to his haul of wins, as he was still considered to be too young to be selected for either the Giro d'Italia or the Tour de France.

Jempi had hoped to be selected for the Belgian team for the World Championships being held in Leicester that year, but his prospects didn't look good, due to his lack of results. However, he came third in the Belgian Championships behind Eddy Merckx and Herman Van Springel, leading to his selection for the team. His form improved as the season progressed, and he was coming into great condition just at the right time, as he won a stage of Paris–Luxembourg in the week preceding the Worlds.

The 1970 World Championships were being held in Mallory Park motor racing circuit in Leicestershire in England. It wasn't a particularly tough lap, but there was quite a strong wind that day. The two main favorites for the race were Eddy Merckx, who had been dominant throughout the year, and the Italian Felice Gimondi, who had finished in second place in the Giro d'Italia earlier that season. Nobody reckoned that the up-and-coming Monseré had a chance, but he had a lot of confidence in his own abilities. Annie recounted that she knew he was in shape, as she noticed how he had packed his bags for the trip across the English Channel. "If he had good legs, he always had smart clothes for the reception afterward," she said, "but this was the World Championships. Nobody believed he had a chance."

Merckx had won both the Giro d'Italia and the Tour de France that season, and it was presumed by the Belgian team manager that the remainder of the team would be riding in support of the man from Brussels. However, after he gave his talk at the pre-race meeting, he asked the rest of the team if there were any questions. Jempi spoke up, saying, "There is more than one rider in this team." He might have been considered an upstart if he hadn't shown such indisputable talent.

It was an unusual start to the race, as an early break formed with many of the favorites in it, including Merckx, Gimondi, Herman Van Springel, and Gianni Motta. However, this break was quickly brought back. A counterattacking group broke away shortly afterward, and this would turn out to be the winning break. Included were Gimondi, the Englishman Les West, the French pair of Charles Rouxel and Alain Vasseur, the Dane Leif Mortensen, and Jempi Monseré. They worked well together, and as their gap grew, it became obvious that the winner would emerge from this group.

It was clear to Gimondi that Monseré was the man he needed to be most concerned about. Mortensen alleged that on the last lap, Gimondi approached the Belgian, apparently offering him thirty-eight thousand guilders to let him win. However, Jempi was very confident of his own abilities, asking the Italian in turn, "How much should I pay you to win?" Les West confirmed afterward that he saw them speaking to each other, but couldn't hear what was said.

Coming into the last few kilometers, Gimondi attacked early but was dragged back by the others. Jempi then counterattacked with five hundred meters to go. Les West recalled that "Monseré was outstanding, he jumped and left us all standing." The Belgian held on to win from Mortensen and Gimondi, becoming the second-youngest World Champion after his compatriot Karel Kaers, who had won the title in 1934. After the race, an emotional Merckx was one of the first of his team to congratulate him.

Fans were ecstatic with his win, and he was immediately signed up to attend a multitude of criteriums, receptions, and various other events. In fact, he clocked up twenty thousand kilometers driving around Europe in the two months after his win.

But misfortune was to strike Jempi not long after he pulled on the famous tunic. His father, Achilles, had a weak heart, and had been told by doctors to refrain from drinking alcohol. However, in Leicester, he had a few beers the evening of his son's win to celebrate his victory. Ten days later, he died from a cardiac arrest. It would be the first of a number of tragedies for the family.

Jean-Pierre tried to put the loss of his father out of his mind as best as he could, and trained particularly hard that winter. He mostly rode alone, and it seemed that he may have found his time on the bike to be cathartic. He did go out on the bike with others occasionally, though, and one of his training partners was another up-and-coming cyclist, Freddy Maertens. Jempi introduced Maertens to Annie's cousin, Carine Brouckaert, and the couple would go on to get married. Maertens remembered that Jempi tried to play mind games with rival cyclists by nurturing a reputation for not taking his training too seriously. However, this was far from the truth, as Maertens recalled Jempi going out for a couple of hours' training prior to meeting up with the other cyclists. "He would also claim that he didn't feel like going training on particular days, and as soon as the others departed, would change into his gear, and head off by himself," said Maertens.

Despite numerous invites for the new World Champion to attend various receptions, football matches, and other events over the winter both in Belgium and abroad, Monseré was still able to find the time to put in a lot of kilometers.

His hard winter's training paid off early in the 1971 season when he won a couple of stages in the Ruta del Sol in February in southern Spain. He looked likely to have another successful season. One of Jempi's early-season targets was Milan–San Remo, and the nature of the course suggested that it was a race that would have suited him.

His last warm-up race prior to traveling to Italy was scheduled to be the Grote Jaarmarktprijs in Retie. His best friend, Roger De Vlaeminck, came to meet him that morning, as Jempi had offered him a lift to the race. When he went out the front door, it was the last time that Annie would see her husband alive. "I went to see him leave with Roger. He was joking at the door. If those two were together, there would always be laughing," she recalled.

The Grote Jaarmarktprijs was considered by most of the top riders to be just a training race, and Jempi was more concerned with the forthcoming Milan–San Remo. Despite this, he still managed to make it into the breakaway group. Halfway through the race, as the leaders turned onto the road from Lille to Gierle, a local woman traveling in the opposite direction apparently ignored police warnings to stop. With the wind now behind them, the riders were reaching a speed estimated at sixty kilometers per hour.

Raphaël Hooyberghs of the Geens-Watney team was at the front of the group, with Jempi on his wheel. Hooyberghs saw the car at the last minute and just about managed to avoid colliding with the oncoming Mercedes. Jempi was tucked closely behind Hooyberghs and couldn't avoid the car. He flew over the hood and smashed into the windshield. His team manager Noël Foré was first to attend to him and said later: "The riders who saw him lying there thought he was unconscious, but I immediately saw he was dead." Photographs of the incident show Foré trying to attend him while Roger De Vlaeminck looks on helplessly.

Jean-Pierre Monseré lies fatally injured while his good friend
Roger De Vlaeminck looks on helplessly.

The driver of the car, Josephine Lammens, remained motionless behind the steering wheel, such was her state of shock. An ambulance was quickly on the scene, but there was nothing they could do. Annie Monseré was at home, packing Jempi's suitcase for Italy, when she heard some bad news. "Around three o'clock, a message came on the radio that the World Champion had crashed. We did not at first know who it was, as Belgium had two World Champions at that time." (World Cyclo Cross Champion Eric De Vlaeminck was the other.) She feared the worst, and her fears were soon confirmed.

The accident shocked other riders who had been in the break. Roger De Vlaeminck recalled, "It was terrible. I had to take his car back home, but I was in a daze. I couldn't believe it. In fact it took me a long time to accept it." Likewise, Frans Verbeeck had difficulty coming to terms with the accident, and has said that he has never been able to forget the noise of the impact.

Thirty thousand people attended the funeral the following weekend. Jempi's coffin was carried by friends and teammates including Roger De Vlaeminck and Joop Zoetemelk. Eddy Merckx won Milan–San Remo on the day of the funeral, and laid his winning bouquet on the grave of his compatriot the following day. Freddy Maertens would repeat the gesture after winning the Belgian title a few months later.

After the death of Monseré, cycling journalists started to ask whether the rainbow jersey was cursed.

Many pointed the finger at Josephine Lammens, but Jempi's mother, Helene, did not believe she was to blame, as Lammens told her that she had not been stopped by any signalman. The grieving mother visited her after the accident. "A few months later I go see this woman," Helene recollected, "she was in a bad way, and I wanted to tell her that her not to blame herself. We embraced, crying uncontrollably, trying to comfort each other."

Monseré's team manager, Briek Schotte, also must have looked back at the accident with regard to the life-changing decision he made for his protégé: Schotte had persuaded Monseré to stay at home in Belgium to prepare for Milan–San Remo, rather than competing at Paris–Nice, which he had originally been penciled in to do.

Unfortunately, that was not the end of the tragedies for the Monseré family. For Giovanni's First Communion, he had been given a bicycle by Freddy Maertens. However, Freddy added some conditions. If he was out riding his bicycle, he had to wear a helmet, and also one of his dad's rainbow jerseys, so that everybody would know who he was. That summer, Freddy was competing in the Tour de France. Giovanni watched him on TV winning a stage, and afterward decided to go out cycling with his friends. Tragically, the young boy was killed when a motorist reversed into him. Maertens's team manager, journalists, and wife Carine somehow managed to keep the news from him, and he stayed in the Tour.

Maertens won two more stages following Giovanni's death, but doubted he could have gotten those victories if he had heard the tragic news, recounting in his biography, "I still feel grateful for that to this day, because I wonder what would have happened to my concentration on the final two stages if things had been different, especially since Giovanni's accident had happened on a racing cycle that he had received from me." Maertens felt enormous guilt visiting Annie Monseré afterward, saying, "Annie was lying in a daze on a settee in the living room. As for me, I was so distressed that I couldn't bring myself to go and see her at first, so Carine tried to comfort her while I stayed in the kitchen."

Years later, Annie gave an interview on TV, where she spoke of the ongoing pain of losing her husband and son. "I can't explain it," she said, "except to say that it must be something more powerful than me, more powerful than any human soul. I can only assume that it's because I was too happy, that I had been blessed. Through all the years, I have never heard anybody speak ill of Jempi, and his son, my boy, was a treasure."

Annie would eventually go on to marry again, and give birth to another son, but still visits the graves of Jempi and Giovanni regularly. A monument now sits at the spot on Turnhoutsebaan in Sint-Pieters-Lille where Jempi lost his life. He was the first of many Belgian cyclists to be given the title "the next Eddy Merckx," and even Merckx himself would concur. He would later say, "Jempi was a big champion. Unbelievable. An immense talent. Without his tragic accident, I'm sure he would have been as good as De Vlaeminck. Maybe he would even have been better than me."

Unlike many other "next Eddy Merckxes," there is little doubt that Jempi could have rivaled his compatriot. By dying so young, however, the question of whether he could have handled the pressure unfortunately just gets added to the long list of unanswered questions in the sport.

7

Drugs, Beer, and Big Gears

Yet another in the production line of Belgian wunderkinds arrived on the scene in the early 1970s in the shape of Freddy Maertens, who would go on to become a two-time winner of the World Championships. The difference between his two reigns in the rainbow jersey was stark. After his 1976 win, he went on to win a multitude of races, including an incredible thirteen stages and the overall in the Vuelta a España, Paris–Nice, Het Volk, and numerous other events. However, following his second Worlds victory, Maertens had a nightmare season the subsequent year, justifying his depiction as a victim of the curse.

Maertens was born in the coastal town of Nieuwpoort to hard-working parents, who between them ran both a grocery and a laundry. He showed a talent in school for languages, and would go on to learn French, English, and Italian in addition to his native Flemish. He also excelled at sports, and would start bike racing at the age of fourteen. He admitted that he struggled with bunch riding to begin with, but by September of that year he had won his first race. He progressed through the ranks rapidly after that.

As mentioned previously, Freddy Maertens had been a great

friend of Jean-Pierre Monseré. It was the year of his elder compatriot's tragic death that saw Maertens's breakthrough. He won the Belgian Amateur title and was second in the World Amateur Road Race, and these performances helped him to gain a professional contract. He held off, though, until after the Olympics in Munich, where he finished in thirteenth position.

He joined the Flandria team directly after the Games, where he was under the tutelage of the great Briek Schotte, "the Last of the Flandrians." Schotte had been another Belgian World Champion, and was able to provide Maertens with some great advice. He was successful from the start as he won one of his first-ever professional races, in Zwevezele.

His success continued in 1973: In only his second year as a pro, he nearly won the World Championship title. The race that year was being held in Montjuich in Barcelona, and was won by the Italian Felice Gimondi. Maertens's Belgian teammate Eddy Merckx claimed afterward that he would have won had Maertens not chased him down on the last lap. Maertens countered that Merckx had not helped him, either, as Merckx was using Campagnolo components, while Maertens used Shimano. Maertens said that two days before the race, the founder of the Italian company, Tullio Campagnolo, drove alongside the Belgian and Italian teams —both training on the circuit—and shouted, "Sort it out between you but Shimano mustn't be allowed to win the championship." This was the dictat that influenced the race. For years afterward, Merckx and Maertens hardly spoke, but they have since put their differences aside.

Maertens's first success in the World Championships came three years later at Ostuni in Italy. His win in the 1976 race had been predicted by many beforehand. Already that season, he had won Ghent–Wevelgem, the Four Days of Dunkirk, and the Belgian Championships, among other races. Once again it seemed the only thing that might have prevented him from taking the title was discontent within the Belgian team. Both Merckx and Maertens felt that they should be the protected rider. On the day of the race, however, the team worked well to give Maertens the opportunity he deserved.

Coming into the finishing straight, Maertens and the Italian Francesco Moser had a narrow lead over the chasers. Moser tried to sneakily get clear by getting in the slipstream of a TV motorbike, but the Belgian chased him down. After he caught Moser, Maertens later claimed that the Italian had offered him ten million francs if he let him win in front of his own crowd, but Maertens turned him down. Moser led out the sprint, but he was no match for Maertens, who easily overtook him to claim his first world title at the age of twenty-four. His first reign in the rainbow colors was a success from the start: He won both the Championship of Flanders and the Grand Prix des Nations shortly after claiming the world title.

He continued where he left off at the start of the following season as he won Het Volk, Paris–Nice, and Vuelta a España. However, he also encountered some issues that would see the start of his fall from grace. His problems started when he failed a doping test after winning La Flèche Wallonne by over four minutes. The victory was taken away from him after he tested positive for the amphetamine Stimul.

His problems continued when he fell and broke his wrist in the Giro d'Italia. But for the break he might have gone on to win the race, as he'd already taken seven stage wins. His seasons after 1977 were equally disappointing. In 1978, he won Het Volk and the Four Days of Dunkirk again but not a lot else. The following seasons were even worse with just two small criterium wins in 1979, and no wins in 1980. Despite being just twenty-eight years of age, it appeared that his best years were behind him.

Many rumors started to circulate about Maertens and the reasons for his tremendous downfall. Maertens himself when asked about his poor results was unable to provide a satisfactory answer. It was said by some that he had a drinking problem. His team manager at Flandria, Lomme Driessens, was to say, "Too much wine and not enough riding, that's his problem."

In 1979, he decided to visit doctors in the United States to see if they could find out what the problem was. While on his trip Stateside, he had a very narrow escape. On the flight to New York, Maertens commented to his friend Paul de Nijs that there seemed to be a strange noise coming from one of the engines. They disembarked at JFK Airport in New York, and the plane continued on to Chicago. Shortly after takeoff from Chicago, one of the engines of the DC-10 fell off the wing. American Airlines Flight 191 crashed near the end of the runway, killing all 271 people on board. It remained the worst air disaster in US history until September 11, 2001.

After a few disastrous seasons and his discussions with doctors in the United States, Maertens seemed to be finding the form that had been eluding him. His comeback as a contender would be equally as surprising as his downfall in the first place. He reemerged as a race winner in the 1981 Tour de France, where he notched up five stage wins, taking the green jersey in the process. This sudden revival in his career resulted in even more rumors being spread about the man from Nieuwpoort.

Maertens attributed his reemergence as a contender to a change the previous year when he joined a foreign team for the first time. He was signed by the Italian San Giacomo team, where he would race alongside future Worlds winner Moreno Argentin. He later told the journalist Alastair Hamilton that "they prepared me very well, training and living like a sportsman has to do."

The World Championships in 1981 were being held in Prague, in what was then Czechoslovakia. Among the favorites were the Italians Giuseppe Saronni and Francesco Moser and Frenchman Bernard Hinault. Saronni had a great sprint and had won a number of stages of the Giro d'Italia earlier that year. Hinault was having an even better season. He had won the Tour de France for the third time, as well as claiming wins in Paris–Roubaix, Dauphiné Libéré, and Amstel Gold. Despite his great form in the Tour de France, not many journalists fancied Maertens's chances.

However, his chance of recapturing the world title nearly didn't come to pass. On the day prior to his departure for Prague, Maertens was involved in a car crash in Belgium while driving to a race. Fortunately, he was uninjured and was able to travel.

Once again, there were problems in the Belgian camp. Maertens felt that there was very little cohesion among the team members, and he didn't expect to receive much support. "I had to do it in Prague helped by only one, Géry Verlinden," he said. Verlinden was his trade teammate from the Boule d'Or team. "Herman Van Springel offered to help Roger De Vlaeminck and Claude Criquielion told us he would be riding in the service of Fons De Wolf."

It was a good thing he did have Verlinden's help: When an early group containing Van Springel went clear, the rest of the Belgian team let the gap grow. This was despite Maertens feeling that his compatriot would not have had a chance if it came down to a sprint. Maertens asked Verlinden to ride to bring this group back, which he did. In the last number of laps, some of the Belgian riders who were still in the leading group approached Maertens and told him that they would be able to help him, in return for some remuneration. Maertens had to bluff them, feigning fatigue.

The Belgian spoke to one of the Italian team, Palmiro Masciarelli, asking what their game plan was. The Italian told him, "If Moser can get away with riders who aren't as fast as him, he becomes our top man. As long as this group stays together, we are all riding for Saronni, and that includes Moser." From this conversation, Maertens knew that Saronni was the man to mark.

Coming toward the finish, the group had been reduced to about thirty riders. The Italians drove the group in a bid to prevent anybody from breaking away—and it worked. As they entered the finishing straight, Saronni's teammate Gianbattista Baronchelli opened up the sprint with Saronni on his wheel. It appeared that the Italian favorite was going to take the win, but Baronchelli eased off with three hundred meters remaining. It was too far for Saronni to sprint into a headwind.

Maertens was on the Italian's wheel and managed to come around him in the last few meters to win by half a wheel, as Hinault took the bronze medal. It was claimed by some afterward that Baronchelli had moved over after realizing that it was Saronni on his wheel rather than Moser.

Maertens would later reveal that he felt that his Worlds win in Prague was the biggest of his career. "It was the most important victory, the most satisfying of my career," he said. "Above all, because for once my wife was there." He received some lucrative contracts

Freddy Maertens narrowly beats Giuseppe Saronni and
Bernard Hinault to take his second world title.

after his win to ride some end-of-season criteriums, and in the fort-night after his victory in Prague, he won some minor races in Bannalec and Sint-Niklaas. These would be his only wins during his second stint in the rainbow jersey.

At the start of the following season, Maertens and his team man-ager, Lomme Driessens, were given an audience with Pope John Paul II in the Vatican. Freddy was surprised to realize that the pope knew who he was and that he was a two-time World Champion. Driessens, on the other hand, was chagrined to not have been given priority when it came to meeting the pope.

Maertens presented him with one of his rainbow jerseys, while in return the pope presented him with four sets of rosary beads. The Belgian may have hoped that the blessing would help ensure that 1982 would be a successful season for him, but it was not to be.

He missed the season's opening race, Het Volk, as a result of trou-ble within his Boule d'Or team. Not long afterward, as he was warming up for the prologue of Tirreno-Adriatico, he cycled into the back of the team car he was riding behind. He was dragged for thirty meters but was able to pick himself up. Badly battered and bruised, Maertens could not finish the race.

In fact, his best result in 1982 was ninth overall in the Three Days of De Panne. Unfortunately, just as things were looking up and he might have had a chance to turn his misfortune around, he was hit three days later by a car during the Tour of Flanders.

His tax problems continued to haunt him. Pol Claeys, the former boss of Maertens's team sponsor Flandria, owed him eight million francs. He had only been paid half of his salary in 1978, and he wasn't paid at all in 1979. The fact that he never received the money from Claeys did not deter the tax authorities, who pursued Maertens. "Well I had to pay taxes on this money, money that I never even received," he explained later. He ended up spending more and more time with his accountant and lawyer, which ate into his training time. The Belgian authorities claimed that he owed them a million dollars, but Maertens reckoned it should have been more like fifty thousand.

Further rumors would abound in the Belgian media about Maertens following his second world title. It was said that he had both drug and drinking problems. Regarding the stories of alcoholism, Maertens recounted his side of the story in his autobiography, *Fall from Grace*.

"I admit that during that period when I was up to my neck in tax problems, I looked for consolation in a good strong drink. Sometimes instead of having a glass or two of wine with a meal I would drink the whole bottle."

His wife, Carine, would try to reason with him. "That's no solution," she would say, "your problems won't have disappeared tomorrow." Freddy continued: "I have never felt like an alcoholic but just a social drinker. Anyway, I've had to carry a reputation as a boozer with me throughout my career.

"My notorious reputation as a drinker dates back to when I won my first world title in Ostuni and signed a publicity contract with the French company, Lanson, in exchange for a thousand bottles of champagne," Maertens went on to say. "The fact that I sold a large number of bottles to Briek Schotte among others was of little interest to the public. As far as they were concerned, Maertens was on the champagne from nine in the morning."

Others claimed that Maertens's problems stemmed from overuse of drugs. He would fail a number of tests throughout his career, including one for Pemoline, an amphetamine, in 1974. Some journalists also felt that Maertens's issues on the bike stemmed from his habit of using big gears, which caused him to burn out. He countered this by claiming that using bigger gears allowed him to descend without putting too much strain on his heart. It was a reflection of the microscopic surveillance that cyclists in Belgium receive—which those in other countries are free of—that his every move was scrutinized by the media.

Maertens reluctantly lined up at the Worlds to defend his crown in 1982 in the second hosting of the event in Great Britain at Goodwood. Once again he courted controversy, when a miscommunication about travel arrangements resulted in him having to get a taxi from Heathrow Airport to the team hotel. Maertens persuaded the taxi driver to stop at a pub on the way and have a beer with him. The reason he gave later was that it was a hot day, and he wanted to cool down. As usual, this incident was reported in the Belgian press as the reigning World Champion having turned up intoxicated at the team hotel. Maertens retired early from the race, and afterward his soigneur turned up at his room with a bottle of champagne, which he would normally have poured into one of his drinking bottles. The two finished off the bottle in a toast to what would be his final Worlds appearance.

His only wins after his second world title were in some minor criteriums. He became somewhat of a journeyman, moving around various small teams in Belgium and the Netherlands. In 1985, he won the last race of his career, a small kermesse in Gistel, a short distance from where he'd grown up. He would fail another drug test in 1986, this time for cortisone, and he would finally hang up his wheels in 1987 after deciding during a training ride that he had simply had enough of the rain and wind of Flanders.

It would take years for Maertens to finally pay off the tax authorities. Even after retirement, his name would continue to be linked with drug problems within the sport. He was particularly incensed when Belgian TV used his photograph when discussing the subject on a documentary, although he would admit to *L'Équipe* that "like everyone else," he had used amphetamines in round-the-houses races. However, he insisted that he had ridden without drugs in important races, as he knew that he would be tested for them.

These days, you can find Freddy Maertens working at the Centrum Ronde van Vlaanderen in Oudenaarde, the museum dedicated to the Tour of Flanders (ironically enough, a race he didn't win). He never forgave Pol Claeys, whom he said was "not a good guy, he promised and promised." Such was the level of falling-out that Maertens refused to attend Claeys's funeral in 2011. Maertens is today back on his feet again and has at last paid off the last of his tax bill after thirty years.

8

Stephen Roche

Despite numerous World Champions struggling during their reign in the rainbow colors, only one rider since World War II has gone through the entire season without any victories. The Irish cyclist Stephen Roche achieved this ignominious feat following his victory in the 1987 race. It was a massive disappointment after the stellar year he'd enjoyed the previous season.

In the mid-1980s, Ireland had just four cyclists plying their trade in the European peloton, but to say that the country punched above its weight at the time is somewhat of an understatement. In Ireland, cycling would have been considered a minor sport, with limited numbers competing. That was to change at the start of the 1980s. Sean Kelly topped the UCI World Rankings from their inception in 1984 through to 1988, and had won nearly all of the major one-day classics. His compatriot Stephen Roche, however, although very talented, could not find the same level of consistency. He had an incredible start to his career, as he won Paris–Nice in his debut season, but had suffered numerous injuries in subsequent years.

It seemed that he might have joined the list of cyclists who never really fulfilled the promise they had initially shown. That was until his *annus mirabilis* in 1987. That year, he would join Eddy Merckx as one of only two cyclists to ever have won the Giro d'Italia, Tour de France, and World Championships in the same year.

Like others before and after him, though, he would endure the worst year of his career while wearing the rainbow stripes. The troubles that caused such a disastrous season dated back to a knee injury that occurred back in 1985. In the Tour de France of that year, he had shown that he was a genuine contender when he finished in third place. Bernard Hinault retired from the sport at the end of the season, so Roche was expected to be one of the favorites the following year. In November, however, he was taking part in the Paris Six-Day at the Bercy track along with the British rider Tony Doyle when he crashed heavily. He was handing over to Doyle to compete for the final sprint in the Madison when his back tire blew out and he fell. A number of other riders then collided with Roche.

Despite a sore knee, he was able to continue, and the pair went on to finish in second place overall. After the Six-Day, Roche rested for a few weeks before resuming training for the 1986 season in January. He had moved to a new team for the new season, Carrera, and was going to be one of its protected riders. As soon as he started training, he realized that the injury was more serious than he first thought.

Some critics said that he had no business competing in the six-day race, but top road riders were offered lucrative contracts for appearing at end-of-season track events. He saw a doctor in Italy who diagnosed his injury as a damaged knee cartilage. He was operated on in April of that year, but the knee was still sore afterward. Carrera entered him in the Giro d'Italia, but he suffered and abandoned with a few stages remaining. He started the Tour de France shortly afterward when he shouldn't have, and struggled to the end in Paris where he finished in forty-eighth place overall. He had missed his opportunity of becoming the first English-speaking winner of the Tour de France—Greg Lemond grabbed that honor instead.

He visited another doctor in Paris at the end of the season, and this time he was diagnosed with fibrosis of the tendon. He was operated on again, and was able to start training again shortly. This time it felt different, though. Unlike his previous operation, he experienced no pain afterward when he cycled.

It seemed that Roche may have turned the corner, as his 1987 season started off very well—he came very close to winning both Paris–Nice and Liège–Bastogne–Liège. The wins did eventually start coming as he took victory in the Tour of Romandy. At the Giro d'Italia, it was expected that he would work to help his teammate Roberto Visentini, who had won the previous year's edition. However, the race proved to be one of the most divisive Grand Tours in a number of decades. Roche took the pink jersey from Visentini, which did not go down well with the *tifosi*.

For the remainder of the race, he had to endure a torrent of abuse from the Italian fans. He was threatened and spat at; he even suspected that his bike had been sabotaged at one stage. He overcame all of these difficulties in the end to become the first English-speaking winner of the Giro. For many, his results thus far that season would have been more than satisfactory, but he had his eyes on the biggest prize of all, the Tour de France. He rested for a few weeks before traveling to Berlin for the start.

There were no obvious favorites for the Tour that year, as five-time winner Bernard Hinault had retired and the winner the previous year, Greg Lemond, had nearly been killed in a hunting accident and was still recovering. It would end up being one of the most open races in years, with the yellow jersey changing hands numerous times. Roche started off well, finishing in third place in the opening prologue in Berlin, and then winning the first long time trial of the race at Futuroscope. Various challengers such as Jean-François Bernard and Charly Mottet fell by the wayside, until it was just down to Roche and the Spaniard Pedro Delgado.

On the stage to Villard-de-Lans, Roche took the yellow jersey for the first time, but he held on to it for just one stage, as Delgado wrestled it from him on the climb to Alpe d'Huez the next day. It seemed that Delgado was destined to take the overall win, as he pulled clear of Roche on the climb to La Plagne. Roche trailed him by over a minute at one stage, but clawed his way back to finish just a handful of seconds behind. Delgado still held the yellow jersey, but his lead wasn't big enough. Roche took it over from Pedro Delgado in the final time trial. He won overall in Paris by just forty seconds.

Following on from the Tour, Roche took part in a number of criteriums back in Ireland. However, he crashed toward the end of one of the races in Cork, landing on the same knee that he had hurt two years previously. Despite the pain, he was still confident of being able to turn in a good ride at the World Championships.

He had struggled with motivation after the Tour, and instead traveled to Austria with the aim of helping his teammate Kelly win the race. Both Irishmen had come close in the past, as both had won medals at the World Championships. Kelly had claimed the bronze medal in Goodwood, England, in 1982, and Roche did the same in Altenrhein, Switzerland, the following year. The circuit seemed to be better suited to a strong sprinter like Kelly. Eddy Merckx had predicted before the race that it would be won by a sprinter, which seemed to be the common consensus.

Roche and Kelly trained with the rest of their small five-man team in the days preceding the race, and these days together helped to build the spirit that would come to the fore during the race. Paul Kimmage, Martin Earley, and Alan McCormack made up the rest of the team. The riders woke up on the morning of the race to torrential rain, which would have suited both Kelly and Roche, as neither rode particularly well in the heat. The circuit was just twelve kilometers long, so they would have to face twenty-three laps. Given the slippery conditions, the Irish riders stayed near the front of the bunch so as to stay out of trouble. The race was the usual war of attrition, but despite numerous riders being dropped as the laps went on, with just one circuit remaining there were still about seventy riders in the lead group.

At the start of that last lap, a number of riders went clear. Roche helped to bridge the gap with Kelly on his wheel. The new lead group contained just seven riders, including the two Irishmen. Roche put in a strong effort to pull this group clear, but others were to get across, including a number of danger men such as Canadian Steve Bauer, and the previous year's winner, Moreno Argentin. The lead group swelled to thirteen riders, and they started to work well together.

Roche continued to do the lion's share of the work at the front as he chased down attacks by Dane Rolf Sørensen and Dutchman Teun van Vliet. However, when he bridged across to Van Vliet, there was no sign of Kelly. The group had split, and Roche was now clear with four others. In addition to van Vliet and Sørensen, the group also contained Guido Winterberg of Switzerland and German Rolf Gölz. Roche was hesitant to work, looking behind for his compatriot. There were only a handful of kilometers left, though, and it didn't look like Kelly would make it back.

Roche later described the moment in his biography, *The Agony and the Ecstasy*: "I looked behind and could see they were stalling. I became anxious. I wondered what was happening. How could Kelly lose contact at this stage? What I did not know was that Kelly and Argentin were having their own private battle of nerves, Kelly refusing to lead the pursuit of a breakaway group that included his teammate, Argentin refusing to lead Kelly because he feared Kelly would then beat him in the sprint."

Coming into the finishing straight, Roche seized his chance and attacked through a narrow gap against the barriers. Winterberg hesitated for a split second to follow him through that gap—and that's all it took. He was now clear.

He described those final moments later, saying, "With about 500 meters left I took one last look behind and decided that Kelly's group was not coming back in time and so I prepared for the attack. The remarkable thing was that there was still something in my legs and when I went I tried to use every available ounce of energy. I was turning a big gear when I attacked and just kept turning it."

There was a rise to the finish line. The chasing group had now caught the four others, and it seemed that they might catch the slowing Roche. However, he just managed to hang on ahead of Argentin and Juan Fernández of Spain. He said, "After about 300 meters I glanced under my arm and got the most beautiful surprise of my life. The others were well behind me and I was going to be World Champion. I kept turning my big gear but close to the line the incline got a little more severe and I struggled through the last 50 meters. But, by then, it did not matter. I was not going to be overtaken."

Stephen Roche hangs on to win the 1987 World Championships.
He would struggle with injuries afterward.

The original team plan had been to set up Kelly for the win, but that didn't matter now: Kelly was also overjoyed, throwing his hands up as he crossed the line in fifth place. Roche would reveal later on, "Even though I went to the World Championships expecting nothing, I now believe that my performance in Villach was the best single-day effort of my career. I don't think I have ever ridden better in my life."

The team celebrated at their hotel that night, and were joined by many of the Irish supporters who had traveled over. Roche was still only twenty-seven years old, so it seemed that he could be expected to win more Grand Tours and possibly even some classics. However, it was not to be.

Prior to the World Championships, he had signed for the Spanish team Fagor. They allowed him to bring with him some riders whom he particularly rated. From the outset, though, Roche realized that the team's organization was chaotic. There was dissent between the team managers, the riders were unhappy with the management, and—to compound matters for Roche—his knee problems were flaring up again.

He visited numerous specialists, but none could correctly diagnose what was wrong with the joint. Three months after capturing the world title, he underwent an operation to have calcium scraped off the tendon on the outside of his knee. The operation didn't work, and the pain persisted.

At Fagor's first training camp, the World Champion was unable to cycle without pain. He went to see other doctors, but they were unable to sort out the problem. Fagor wanted him to take part in the Vuelta or the Giro, but he was unable to start either. Likewise, he was unable to defend his Tour de France title.

That year, Roche met with Dr. Hans-Wilhelm Müller-Wohlfahrt, the doctor at the soccer club Bayern Munich. Having been misdiagnosed by a number of specialists previously, Roche was somewhat skeptical about being analyzed by yet another doctor. Müller-Wohlfahrt did have an excellent reputation, though, having worked with numerous football and rugby players, golfers, and other athletes. He would even work with the lead singer of U2, Bono, to help with his back problems.

The German doctor was able to successfully diagnose what had happened to Roche, and helped to rebuild the muscle around his knee over the winter of 1988–89. The rehabilitation worked, and he seemed to be getting back to his best at the start of the following season. However, despite winning the Tour of the Basque Country, his struggles with Fagor continued, and he suffered further injuries to his back and knee. He moved from team to team after 1989, winning a handful of races, but he never came close to regaining the form he had shown in the year of his triple crown.

He finally retired in 1993 having finished in ninth place at the Giro and thirteenth place in the Tour. He gave an emotional TV interview on the Champs-Élysées at the end of the Tour, as it suddenly seemed to dawn on him that his time as a professional cyclist was at an end. He would subsequently go to work as a commentator, in addition to running training camps.

Roche would speak about his year as World Champion and his attitude toward the curse of the rainbow jersey in his autobiography, *Born to Ride*. "I can understand why many people have pointed to my year as World Champion as evidence that there is something to that phenomenon, but it's not something that I really think about. I recognize that my season as the World Champion was almost a total write-off and that if luck had been with me I could perhaps have won another Tour."

Roche was quite pragmatic about his disappointing year, and he didn't let his knee problems get him down as he said, "If I hadn't had my knee problems that year, I might have suffered some other setback, perhaps something even more serious."

9

Big in Japan

More often than not, the World Championships are won by one of the favorites, but occasionally one of the less fancied riders takes the honors. In 1990, the Belgian Rudy Dhaenens became one of those riders. The man from Deinze in East Flanders had been selected as one of the riders to support their team leader, Claude Criquielion, in his bid to win the rainbow jersey again, having taken the honors in 1984 and come close in 1988. Instead, Dhaenens became the unlikely winner of the title.

Dhaenens had turned professional in 1983, joining Criquielion on the Splendor-Euroshop team. He had a solid but unspectacular first few seasons in the professional ranks, and despite finishing on the podium of both Paris–Roubaix and the Tour of Flanders, the big classic win had eluded him. Dhaenens had taken a stage in the 1986 Tour de France, and he came close to a second one in the 1989 race. On the last corner, however, his tubular tire rolled off his rim, and he crashed to the ground. He was as well known for this near miss as he was for any of his wins.

He would say afterward, "I'm always in the top group, usually in the front, but never win. And that's what's important in cycling races. To win, you need luck." It was that elusive luck he seemed to be missing.

In 1990 it appeared that he may have turned a corner, as that season was proving to be one of his most consistent. He had been given the opportunity to lead the PDM team during the spring classics because their usual team leader, Sean Kelly, had broken his collarbone after crashing heavily on the first stretch of cobbles in the Tour of Flanders. Dhaenens showed that he was well capable of stepping up to the mark: He escaped with Moreno Argentin in the latter stages of the race, only to be outsprinted by the Italian for the win. He achieved another good placing the following week as he finished in ninth place in Paris–Roubaix. His good form continued throughout the season, and he would go on to have his career-best result in the Tour de France, finishing in forty-third position overall.

The World Championships that year were being held for the first time in Asia, as there was growing awareness within the UCI that they needed to increase the globalization of the sport. Utsunomiya—120 kilometers north of Tokyo—was selected as the venue. Prior to the event, there had been concerns about holding the championships in Japan, given the heat and humidity, along with the travel distances. Some also worried that this alien sport would not grab the attention of the Japanese public, but in the end spectators flocked in droves to see the best cyclists in the world compete in their country.

The professionals would have to negotiate eighteen laps of a 14.5-kilometer circuit to total 261 kilometers. Among the favorites for the race were Greg Lemond, Sean Kelly, Gianni Bugno, and Pedro Delgado. None of the Belgians was seen as a serious threat, least of all Dhaenens.

The lap included a 1.8-kilometer climb, Mount Kogashi in Utsunomiya Forest Park, but the summit was 10 kilometers from the end of the lap, which would give dropped riders enough distance to regain the leaders if they were distanced the last time up the climb.

The usual early break went clear in the race, containing twenty-two riders. Their lead went up over six minutes at one stage, before the bunch started to draw them back. Compared with other World Championships, there was quite a high rate of attrition—only 57 of the original 145 starters would go on to finish the race.

The descent from the climb was particularly slippy, and one casualty was the Norwegian Dag Otto Lauritzen. He was uninjured, however, and able to make his way back to the group with all the favorites. On the fourth-to-the-last lap, after all the early breakaways had been brought back, a group of four went clear; Lauritzen then bridged across with the Swiss rider Thomas Wegmüller. On the penultimate climb of Kogashi, Lauritzen attacked again, and Dhaenens's teammate Dirk De Wolf was the only rider able to stay with him.

At one stage on the climb, De Wolf looked back to see Dhaenens coming across. As he sat up and waited for his teammate, De Wolf turned around to call up his team car. However, he somehow wobbled and fell to the ground, taking Lauritzen with him. The Norwegian's chances disappeared when he dropped his chain. He was incensed and actually tried to punch the Belgian. He said afterward, "It was so frustrating. That was the moment of my life to win, and then De Wolf turns and falls in front of me."

The confusion of the crash gave Dhaenens the opportunity he was looking for, and with just eight kilometers remaining, the two Belgians attacked. Accompanying them were Spaniard Alberto Leanizbarrutia and Frenchman Martial Gayant. Going over the top, their lead over the group of favorites was twenty-five seconds. Yet this second group—driven by Bugno, Lemond, and Canadian Steve Bauer—was unable to make inroads into the lead.

The Australian Stephen Hodge somehow did manage to make it across to the four leaders just after they had passed the finish line to start the final lap. He got on to the back of the leaders just as they started the final ascent, but as soon as he did, Dhaenens and De Wolf attacked. The peloton containing the main favorites did make a belated chase; at one stage, it looked like they might catch them. With just five hundred meters remaining, however, they had only reduced the gap by ten seconds. De Wolf lead out the sprint but was easily overtaken by his compatriot in the last few meters for the biggest win of his career. Eight seconds later, Gianni Bugno won the bunch sprint narrowly from Greg Lemond to claim the bronze medal. Lemond revealed afterward that he felt that the course hadn't been difficult enough and that Dhaenens had ridden a very smart race.

Afterward, Dhaenens revealed that he thought at one stage they would be caught: "When Dirk told me with one kilometer to go that he had cramps all I thought of was who would catch us. I urged him on to work with all he had. Finally, it was my turn to win but I've learned to become patient."

Shortly after his return to Europe, Dhaenens suffered misfortune when a tendon strain forced him to cancel his start for the team in the Grand Prix de la Libération team time trial, which PDM duly won. However, he bounced back in the Canadian round of the World Cup and in one of his final races of the season, the Grand Prix des Amériques, he finished eighth.

It seemed that Dhaenens could now be considered a genuine classics contender. Given the depth of the PDM team, he would have more opportunities elsewhere. One of the teams that expressed interest in him was the Dutch team Panasonic. Dhaenens signed a lucrative contract with PDM's rivals for the next two seasons, and their team manager, Peter Post, firmly believed that he would be the man to help them in the northern classics.

His 1991 season started well, as he partnered with fellow Belgian Etienne De Wilde to victory in the Six Days of Antwerp. His spring classics campaign was a disaster, though: He recorded no results. The main reason he had been signed by Panasonic was that he'd finished in the top five in both the Tour of Flanders and Liège–Bastogne–Liège the previous season. It seemed like he may have turned a corner at the Tour de France when he finished in fourth place on the opening road stage, but that was as good as it got. His only win that season was in a small criterium in Eeklo.

The following year was even worse, as he recorded no results whatsoever. He was still only thirty-one years old, so he felt that he had time to turn his fortune around and win big again. However, toward the end of the 1992 season, Dhaenens went for what he thought would just be a routine medical checkup. He couldn't believe what the doctor was saying when he was told that he should-n't be riding his bike. The doctor informed him that he was suffering from a serious heart disease.

Dhaenens was not the only cyclist who had raced with PDM who would suffer from heart problems. In February 1990, Dhae-nens's Dutch teammate Johannes Draaijer died suddenly of a heart attack at the age of twenty-seven, seven months after he had fin-

Rudy Dhaenens after winning the 1990 World Championships.
He was diagnosed with heart problems a couple of years afterward.

ished in twentieth position in the Tour de France. He died in his sleep of a heart blockage, just a few days after completing a race in Italy where a doctor had said he was fit to ride. Initially, his death was blamed on "cardiovascular abnormalities," apparently brought on by the stress of the sport. However, Draaijer's wife would later tell the German news magazine *Der Spiegel* that her husband became sick after using the drug erythropoietin, or EPO as it was more commonly known. She hoped that his death would serve as a warning to other cyclists contemplating using the drug. Unfortunately, it didn't.

Another Dutch cyclist, Danny Nelissen, had turned professional with PDM in 1990. Four years later, Nelissen was forced to retire as a professional due to "heart rhythm impairments." He returned the following year to win the World Amateur Championships before finally retiring at the age of twenty-eight due to further heart problems.

It seems more than coincidental that three members of the PDM team from 1990 suffered serious heart problems. In 1991, the year after Dhaenens had moved to Panasonic, the PDM team had mysteriously withdrawn from the Tour de France, and it was initially said that the entire team was suffering from food poisoning. However, their team manager Wim Sanders would later reveal in a TV documentary that the cause for the withdrawal was the incorrect storage of Intralipid, a fat emulsion used to aid nutrition. It was also later alleged that Sanders had supplied riders with anabolic steroids and EPO.

The director for the Netherlands Center for Doping Affairs (NeCeDo), Emile Vrijman, would later reveal details of a conversation that had taken place at those World Championships in Japan.

According to Vrijman, a doctor from the American EPO producer Amgen intimated that his colleague from the Belgian division of the company had suggested that EPO was being widely used by the Belgians in a race where they took both first and second places.

Former PDM manager Manfred Krikke would admit, "We were not the most ethical team in the peloton. We were just on the edge. But the directions from the PDM company was that there were to be no 'doping affairs' not that 'there was to be no drugs.'"

The reason EPO usage leads to heart failure is that the drug increases the number of red blood cells, which in turn raises the blood's viscosity. This causes blood to clot more easily. Thicker blood increases the chances of a heart attack or stroke. Heart attacks in cyclists often occurred in the middle of the night, when resting heart rates were lowest. It would be widely reported that cyclists were known to ride on stationary bikes during the night to ensure that their blood flowed and didn't clot.

It was said afterward that Dhaenens's heart problems were congenital, but it seems obvious why some commentators would identify a link between EPO usage in the team and the fact that a number of its riders suffered such issues. In addition, numerous deaths of Belgian and Dutch cyclists were said to be attributable to the use of EPO. The Polish rider Joachim Halupczok, who had finished in fourteenth place in Utsunomiya and had won the world amateur title the previous year, was among those rumored to have died from heart problems caused by EPO usage.

Despite the initial upset Dhaenens had gone through after his premature retirement, he adjusted well to life outside the peloton, working as an investment adviser for a brokerage firm. He also established a cycling school in Aalst and became a well-respected cycling commentator for Eurosport.

In 1998, he was driving along the Brussels–Ostend motorway on his way to the end of the Tour of Flanders—a race in which he'd finished second in the same year that he claimed his world title—when he had an accident. He somehow lost control of his car, swerving off the road and into an electrical pole. He was taken to the hospital, where doctors operated on him for hours. He fell into a coma and had to be placed on a ventilator. Despite their best efforts, the following evening he died from his injuries, leaving behind his wife, Greta, and two young children, Claudia and Thibaut.

It was an indication of the esteem that Dhaenens was held in that four of the great Belgian cyclists were among the pallbearers: Eddy Merckx, Freddy Maertens, Claude Criquielion, and Benoni Beheyt. Other great Flandrians such as Briek Schotte, Rik Van Steenbergen, and Rik Van Looy also paid their respects. All seven had also previously been World Champions. It was a mark of the popularity of the Flandrian that many of the mourners were unable to fit into the church; TV screens had to be set up in the nearby marketplace.

On the week that he died, Dhaenens should have been celebrating his thirty-seventh birthday, but he became yet another cyclist whose career seemed to go into free fall following his World Championship win.

10

Luc Leblanc

The structure of professional cycling has always been very different from that of other sports. Compared with other team sports, the life span of a cycling team can be much shorter. They don't own stadiums and require considerably less investment to establish. Therefore, it is not unknown for professional teams to last just a couple of seasons before disappearing. Apart from their short-term contracts, professional cyclists have also always been quite vulnerable when it comes to team owners honoring contracts. In the past few decades, a number of teams have folded without warning, including the Linda McCartney Racing Team in 2001 and Jan Ullrich's team in 2003, sponsored by the Coast clothes retailer. In 1995, another team would collapse, which in turn affected the then World Road Race Champion, Luc Leblanc. It was not the first adversity that Leblanc would have to overcome.

When he was just eleven years old, Leblanc and his younger brother Gilles were hit by a drunk driver. Luc had to stay in the hospital for six months, but unfortunately Gilles died. Luc underwent numerous operations, and was left with one leg weaker and an inch shorter than the other. A physiotherapist recommended that he start cycling as part of the rehabilitation process.

Leblanc came from a devout Catholic family, deciding as a boy that he wanted to become a priest, but when he quickly showed talent on the bike he changed his mind. None other than Raymond Poulidor helped convince him that his future lay in professional cycling. Leblanc would retain his strong beliefs, however, and he became known to some in the peloton as Saint Luc.

He received his first contract with the Toshiba team in 1987, but had a slow start to his career. Only after his move to the Castorama team of Laurent Fignon in 1990 did he emerge as a Tour de France contender, finishing in fifth place overall. In the process, he took the yellow jersey for just one day. He later gave the jersey to his mentor, Poulidor. It looked like he had made the breakthrough, but he continued to be plagued by his old childhood injury, and he struggled to achieve any real level of consistency.

Following a quiet few years, Leblanc came good again in 1994 after another change in teams, this time to Festina. He won the eleventh stage of the Tour de France to Hautacam, ahead of Miguel Indurain and Marco Pantani, and at fourth place overall he just missed out on a podium finish. He also won the mountains classification of the Vuelta a España, helping cement his selection to the French team for the World Championships.

The French had a particularly strong team that year that also included Leblanc's Festina teammates Pascal Hervé, Richard Virenque, and Pascal Lino. Agrigento on the south coast of Sicily had been selected as the venue; the race consisted of nineteen laps of a circuit that included a slope reaching 15 percent at its steepest point.

The team was one of the strongest in the race, but lacked a great sprinter. It was therefore in members' interests to ensure that the race was aggressive, and to try to break it up. Right from the start, French Champion Jacky Durand attacked, but he didn't get anywhere. It did set the tone for the race, though: Numerous riders went up the road, but none of the breaks lasted for any length of time.

On the third last lap, Leblanc infiltrated the decisive break, which contained many of the race favorites. On the penultimate time up the climb, the Frenchman bridged up to the two leaders, Massimo Ghirotto of Italy and Dane Rolf Sørensen. As they started the last lap, they had a small lead of fifteen seconds over the chasers.

One of the favorites for the race was the defending champion, Lance Armstrong. The American had limited success during his year in the rainbow colors, but was still considered to be one of the main contenders for the race, as he seemed to be coming into form. However, he lost contact with the leaders when his chain jumped. His foot came off the pedal, causing him to fall on his handlebars.

On the last lap, Sørensen attacked alone, and on the final climb he was chased by Leblanc and Ghirotto. Five hundred meters from the top of the climb, the Frenchman caught and passed Sørensen, with Ghirotto unable to hold on to his wheel. Behind, Armstrong and the Russian Dimitri Konyshev led the chase, but they were unable to get any help from Richard Virenque or Claudio Chiappucci, who both had teammates up the road.

The chasers could not claw Leblanc back, and he held on to become the first French winner of the World Championships since Bernard Hinault fourteen years previously. Chiappucci grabbed second, nine seconds behind, and Virenque took the bronze medal. It was a reflection of the difficulty of the course that only fifty-seven riders made it to the finish.

Luc Leblanc after winning the World Championships in Sicily.

He had taken easily the biggest win of his career, but what Leblanc did not realize at that stage was that he had also made one of the biggest mistakes of his career. Just days prior to his win in Sicily, Leblanc had signed a contract with a new French team being formed, sponsored by Le Groupement. One of the reasons why he was said to have wanted to leave Festina was his difficult relationship with Virenque.

The previous July, the Groupement organization had decided to invest thirty million francs in sponsoring a cycling team for the following season. The official line was that Le Groupement was a door-to-door sales company, but the truth would turn out to be somewhat different.

Le Groupement was at the center of controversy because its main sponsor, the European Grouping of Marketing Professionals (GEPM), a French company selling multilevel marketing, was the subject of much investigation and criticism by the media. *Multilevel marketing* was said to be a nice term for pyramid selling.

The Festina team that Leblanc was leaving would later become synonymous with the problem of drugs in cycling, but it seemed that there was systematic doping within the team even when Leblanc was there. In Willy Voet's revelatory book on the sport, *Breaking the Chain*, which exposed many of the doping practices in the peloton at the time, he would report the preparations that the Festina riders had made in advance of the 1994 World Championships.

Voet indicated that the riders, including Leblanc, had received a dose of EPO on the Thursday before the race, and that Virenque's hematocrit level was at 52 percent. The UCI would set 50 percent as the maximum allowable hematocrit level for cyclists. Voet went on to say, "And like the three other Festina riders, he had been allowed to have an intramuscular injection of 10 milligrams of Diprostene—

a corticosteroid—the day before the race, and 20 milligrams the morning of the start."

According to Voet, Leblanc had pulled a fast one on Virenque. Coming into the last lap, Virenque had told his teammate that he was going to attack shortly, and could easily put a minute into the group. Shortly afterward, however, it was Leblanc who had attacked instead, knowing that his compatriot would not be able to lead the chase.

The drug taking was supposed to have continued after the race back at the team hotel. The team partied hard to celebrate Leblanc's win, and according to Voet quite a lot of those present took Pot Belge. The notorious cocktail of drugs used by cyclists was said to have contained amphetamines, cocaine, heroin, caffeine, and analgesics. Voet said that it was the first time Leblanc had taken amphetamines. It seemed that it was possibly the right decision to leave Festina.

Following that year's Tour de France, Leblanc had been contacted by Patrick Valcke, who would be one of the directeurs sportifs for the new team. Guy Mollet would be the team manager. Leblanc initially told the Festina manager, Bruno Roussel, that he would be re-signing with his team. He soon backtracked, however, and announced instead that he would be joining Valcke's team.

Le Groupement launched to much fanfare, having also signed a number of other star riders, including the Scot Robert Millar and the Dutch sprinter Jean-Paul van Poppel. They also revealed the jersey the team would wear, which was garish to say the least. It was akin to something that the famous American advocate of psychedelic drugs Dr. Timothy Leary might have designed following one of his experiments.

The new team had a very difficult start to the year. The season hadn't even started when one of their riders was sacked. The Flying Scotsman, Graeme Obree, had broken the world hour record the previous season, and had been signed by the team with the intention of winning the prologue of the 1995 Tour de France, taking the yellow jersey in the process.

Obree had gotten off to a bad start with the team. Along with Robert Millar, he was late for the first team meeting. While there, it was explained to him that two thousand pounds of his salary would be used for "medical back-up." Obree told them that he wouldn't be paying, as he had always looked after himself. He then missed the team get-together at the start of the year and was fired by Patrick Valcke for a "lack of professionalism." He later wondered whether it was his refusal to become involved in the team's medical program that was the real reason for his dismissal.

Obree also noted that there was a bad feeling toward him at the team meeting he had attended. He felt that only one of the French riders on the team had shown any friendliness toward him, and that was Luc Leblanc.

In addition to the internal difficulties within the team, they also struggled to gain any results of note. Valcke acknowledged that they were struggling at the start of the season, saying prior to Liège–Bastogne–Liège, "The team is having some problems at this moment with a lot of riders sick. Now, unhappily, Luc Leblanc is sick. So everything's a little set back. Luc Leblanc has a fever and he's out of the race, which is a big handicap."

When asked as to whether Leblanc had fallen victim to the curse of the rainbow jersey, Valcke responded, "Everybody talks about that. I knew it in '88 when Roche was World Champion and maybe there is a curse and maybe just luck or bad circumstances."

Rumors were also starting to circulate that the team was struggling financially. American journalist Sam Abt was to write of them, "The publicity was mainly unfavorable. French newspapers and television channels looked at the Groupement sales system, which is based on motivational sessions and individual investment in the company's retail goods, and decided it had a cult like aura."

However, Valcke was quick to try to put an end to rumors about his team, saying, "The team is here, it exists. Luc Leblanc has a three-year contract and we'll go to the end of his contract. Period. The discussion is finished. If you know something contrary, tell me. If anybody knows to the contrary, let me know.

"The real problem," Valcke continued, "is that Luc Leblanc is the World Champion and everybody notices when he's sick. Today everybody is interested in Luc Leblanc because he's the World Champion, but have you seen Miguel Indurain yet this season?" The Spanish multiple Tour winner had also had an inauspicious start.

The unease surrounding the team seemed to be affecting the World Champion. It looked like his tenure in the rainbow jersey had reached its nadir in the Trophée des Grimpeurs, a one-day race. There he suffered the ignominy of being lapped by the winner,

Armand De Las Cuevas, eventually coming in over twelve minutes behind.

On June 27, just two days after the various national championship races around Europe, the news came through that the team was folding. It wasn't the greatest-ever surprise. The Tour de France was just a matter of a few days away, but Le Groupement would not be there.

Some team members claimed that they were owed money, and their wages had not been paid. Although most of the riders were able to find new contracts, former Tour de France green jersey winner Jean-Paul van Poppel decided to retire. Another victim was the veteran Scotsman Robert Millar. He had won the British Championships that week, and wouldn't get the opportunity to wear his champion's jersey.

It was the second time that a rainbow jersey wearer had suffered a terrible year under the management of Patrick Valcke, after Stephen Roche's *annus horribilis* in 1988. Maybe it was Valcke who was the jinx rather than the jersey.

Leblanc did manage to get a new contract with the Italian team Polti. However, he suffered further misfortune when he had to undergo surgery on his sciatic nerve, which forced him out of the sport for three months.

Despite winning a stage of the 1996 Tour, Leblanc never achieved the same level in the sport that he had reached the year he won the Worlds. In 1999, he was fired by Polti supposedly because of injury, and he had to take the team to court for unfair dismissal. Leblanc had finished second in that year's French Championships and seventh in the Tour of Romandy, so it did indeed seem odd that Polti had sacked him due to injury. It would later be said that the real reason was that the team had signed Richard Virenque; Leblanc was sacrificed to allow management the budget for signing him.

The following year, in the trial against Richard Virenque, Leblanc would also admit to having taken EPO during his career. The downfall was complete.

As for Le Groupement, it was later revealed that a complaint had been filed against the company by a government-funded French cult advice group, UNADFI (National Union of Associations for the Defense of the Family and the Individual), along with a consumer advice association, the Women's Social and Civic Union, on behalf of around three hundred people who had been left destitute by the company. This complaint led to a police inquiry. A French parliamentary report soon revealed that more telephone inquiries (almost a thousand per year) were being made to UNADFI about Le Groupement than about Scientology.

Le Groupement had been created by Jean Godzich, who had been previously expelled from Amway, an American multilevel marketing company, for unethical behavior. Godzich and twelve of his colleagues steadfastly protested their innocence, but they were eventually charged with operating a pyramid scam.

The company was also successfully sued in the civil courts by its victims, but its declared assets were insufficient to pay its debts. Le Groupement was bankrupted and compulsorily wound up in 1995.

A warrant was issued for the arrest of Jean Godzich, but he had already escaped to the United States with a large amount of cash.

If there was any consolation for Leblanc from his miserable year as World Champion, it was that he never had to wear the garish jersey of Le Groupement when his tenure in the rainbow colors was over. Every cloud has a silver lining, as they say.

11

The Festina Affair

The use of performance-enhancing drugs has always been synonymous with cycling. Since the advent of the sport, there have been rumors of drug use. Performance enhancements may have been introduced in the 1890s with nitroglycerin, which was said to stimulate the heart after a cardiac attack, and was credited with improving a rider's breathing. Riders would suffer hallucinations from the use of the drug, combined with their exhaustion. The American track rider Major Taylor withdrew from one race in New York, saying, "I cannot go on with safety, for there is a man chasing me around the ring with a knife in his hand." In the decades that followed, other drugs would be introduced to the sport, including strychnine, cocaine, caffeine, amphetamines, and testosterone.

However, in the late 1980s a new type of drug was rumored to have been introduced to the peloton. Erythropoietin, or EPO as it's more commonly known, was originally developed to control red blood cell production, and was used to help treat anemia and cancer. It was quickly discovered that it was also extremely beneficial for endurance athletes. A higher percentage of red blood cells in his system would benefit an athlete, as red blood cells transport oxygen to tissues. However, a red blood cell concentration that was too high would put additional strain on his cardiovascular system, and could cause cardiac arrest.

Between 1987, when EPO became available in Europe, and 1990, eighteen Dutch and Belgian cyclists died suddenly, raising suspicions that naive users did not realize they were playing with fire. It wouldn't be until 2000 that a test was developed by the French national anti-doping laboratory, the LNDD, for detecting pharmaceutical EPO and differentiating it from the nearly identical natural hormone. In the intervening years, before testing was possible, its use was rife, and the general public was oblivious to its ubiquity until the Festina Affair in 1998.

Laurent Brochard's background was in running; he didn't start bicycle racing until he was nearly twenty. He quickly showed that he had made the right move, as he won a number of top amateur races in both France and Belgium. He made his professional debut with the Castorama team in 1992, when the use of EPO was becoming more widespread within the peloton. His first few years were solid, if unspectacular, and he was nearly as well known for his image as he was for his performances on the bike thanks to his penchant for wearing bandanas over his mullet haircut.

That would change for Brochard, or La Broche as he was known in France, when he transferred to the Festina team in 1995. This team had the likes of Richard Virenque and Laurent Dufaux on its roster, and Brochard found that he was also given the chance to lead the team when the opportunity arose. What wasn't known at the time was what was going on behind closed doors with the team.

In 1997, Brochard had his biggest victory, when he won a stage of the Tour de France on Bastille Day in Loudenvielle. This win helped to ensure his selection for the French team for the World Championships, being held in San Sebastián later in the year.

Brochard lined up alongside 162 other riders to face 257 kilometers of a circuit that was deemed by many to be not difficult enough. His main aim was to help his trade teammate Richard Virenque as well as Laurent Jalabert to capture the title. Among the other favorites were Johan Museeuw, winner of the title the previous year, Alex Zülle, Michele Bartoli, and Bjarne Riis. Following a delayed start due to protests by Basque separatists, the race followed its usual custom of breaks forming with lesser riders. It was only in the last ninety kilometers that the French and Italian teams moved to the front to try to take control.

On the last lap, a break went clear containing most of the favorites, including Jalabert, Bartoli, and Museeuw. Brochard also managed to infiltrate the break. With five kilometers remaining, the Spaniard Melchior Mauri managed to get clear, taking Brochard with him. The Dutchman Léon van Bon, Denmark's Bo Hamburger, Switzerland's Dufaux, and Udo Bölts of Germany would join up with the leading two. As they passed under the *flamme rouge*, Brochard put in a blistering attack. Van Bon was the only one to get back to him, but just sat on Brochard's wheel. The Frenchman would not be content with silver, so he did not drive the break.

Brochard and van Bon's soft pedaling enabled the other four to come back to them with a few hundred meters left. Van Bon took up the sprint and looked good for the win. However, with one hundred meters remaining, he started to fade, and Brochard came around him to take the win. Van Bon told reporters afterward that Brochard had "played a very smart game," while Hamburger said that "Brochard was just a little stronger than me."

The American cycling journalist Samuel Abt noted that Brochard was "notably reserved at a news conference afterward," and this prompted one journalist to ask him if he realized that he had actually won the World Championships. Brochard replied that he kept his emotions inside. "I'm really quite reserved, but that doesn't mean that I'm not thrilled." His behavior did raise some eyebrows.

Then when he was asked whom he dedicated his victory to, he replied, "First, to me, since I did the work." It seemed almost an afterthought when he added that he also wanted to dedicate the win to his wife, Veronique, and their five-year-old daughter, Lolita.

It capped off a great season for the man from Le Mans, and he could look forward to the following year when he could wear the rainbow jersey with pride. The 1998 season would turn out to be a memorable one for him, but unfortunately it was for all the wrong reasons.

That season started quietly enough for the newly crowned World Champion, but he wasn't overly concerned, as he was aiming to ride strongly later in the year, in the Tour de France. The strategy seemed to be working: It looked like he was coming into form at the right time when he took a stage of the Grand Prix du Midi Libre in June. This ensured his selection for the Tour de France team, if there was ever any doubt.

That year's Tour was making one of its rare forays away from Continental Europe, as it was starting in Dublin. As the teams gathered in the Irish capital, news started to filter through that French customs officers had made a drug seizure from one of the Tour teams near the Belgian border. Three days prior to the Grand Départ, a soigneur from the Festina team, Willy Voet, had been stopped in Neuville-en-Ferrain, where the officers discovered large quantities of anabolic steroids, EPO, and syringes among other doping products.

The Festina directeur sportif, Bruno Roussel, would declare that the drug find had nothing to do with the team. However, the police alleged that they had found documents at the team's headquarters

World Champion Laurent Brochard and teammates Richard Virenque and Laurent Dufaux protest their innocence during the 1998 Tour de France.

outlining systematic doping programs for team members. The Tour started under a dark cloud while Voet remained in custody. After three days racing in Ireland, the entourage returned to France, where upon arrival Roussel was arrested and the team hotel was searched. The following day, Brochard and his teammates held a press conference announcing that they would continue in the race. However, the decision was taken out of their hands, as they were expelled by the Tour director, Jean-Marie Leblanc.

The Tour rumbled on with other teams being thrown off the race amid protests by the remaining cyclists over the police searches that were now being conducted. Brochard and his teammates were taken to hospital to undergo extensive drug tests as more details of the systematic program emerged. On July 24, Brochard and four of his teammates, under increasing pressure, would finally admit to doping. It was a most ignominious end to his reign in the rainbow jersey. Willy Voet would later claim that there were only three riders in the whole Festina squad who were clean: Christophe Bassons, Patrice Halgand, and Laurent Lefèvre.

In November, the results taken from the nine riders were released. Evidence of steroids, corticoids, and human growth hormone had been found in their systems. Brochard had tested positive for synthetic EPO, in addition to having traces of amphetamines present in his samples. His hematocrit level was at 50.3 percent, above the legal limit of 50 percent established the previous year. The following month, he was suspended by the French Cycling Federation for six months; he would be unable to ride until April 30, 1999. Festina stood by Brochard when his suspension was over, but he was subject to a 50 percent pay cut.

That year, Willy Voet would release his tell-all book, *Breaking the Chain*, revealing the systematic doping program at Festina. As he outlined, prior to the French Championships the previous year, on the weekend before the Tour started he helped some of the Festina cyclists charge up. He recounted giving intramuscular injections of cortisone to Hervé, Virenque, Brochard, Didier Rous, and Christophe Moreau. He explained how the drug was administered and how riders could avoid getting caught by the testers, saying "Ten milligrams of Kenacort in one buttock. It can't be detected in the urine. In the case of a blood test, the doctor can ascertain that there is an abnormality, but cannot be certain that the cortisone is exogenous because the suprarenal glands produce it naturally."

Voet also claimed in his book that Brochard was among those on the team who started using the anabolic steroid clenbuterol, and that he tested the growth hormone IGF-1 prior to the 1996 World Championships in Lugano. However, Voet said, Brochard felt it actually slowed him down. Clenbuterol had been developed as a decongestant to help with disorders such as asthma, but was used as a performance-enhancing drug to help build muscle mass. Voet explained that it was expensive, and not much was known about it. He tested it on himself to see how long it would take to pass through his system and become undetectable. With the tests done at the lab in Ghent, Voet reported that it took eight days. Virenque, Hervé, Brochard, and Emmanuel Magnien were started on it in 1997.

The trial into the Festina case opened on October 23, 2000, and Brochard was among those called to the stand. At the trial, the last two riders from the Tour de France who were still claiming to be innocent would finally confess. After two years of strenuous denials, Richard Virenque and Pascal Hervé would finally admit that they were involved in the doping program also.

Virenque's admission was somewhat bizarre, as he said that he had doped unintentionally, and that it had happened without his approval. A French satirical television program would later portray Virenque as an imbecilic puppet with hypodermic syringes stuck in his head. To many observers, it seemed that Virenque was unrepentant.

When asked why the confession had taken him so long, Hervé responded, "It took me 2½ years to say it. But I would have confessed earlier if there had not been just the nine of us idiots caught two years ago on the Tour de France." His implication was that the vast majority of the peloton were taking performance-enhancing drugs.

Brochard would admit during the hearing that he was probably still under the influence of drugs when he won World Championships. He said that there were still "remnants of doping substances" in his body when he was crowned in San Sebastián: "There was some drug taking during the Tour of Spain and it took place 10 days before the World Championships. There was probably some [drugs] left." He denied taking drugs on the actual day of the road race.

In his book, Voet claimed that there had been a cover-up by the UCI president around the championships that year. He said that

Hein Verbruggen "was one of the people who made necessary arrangements to ensure that the doping scandal surrounding Laurent Brochard during the 1997 World Championships in San Sebastian never became public." Voet also reported that Brochard was positive for lidocaine when he was tested at the end of the race. Years later, it would be alleged during the investigation into doping by Lance Armstrong that the UCI had also helped to cover up a positive test result for the American.

This positive result would also be discussed during the trial, where it emerged that Brochard had obtained a medical certificate to clear his name. Bruno Roussel alleged that the UCI had given Brochard the name of a doctor who could forge the certificate. Roussel's lawyer would later say, "The trial raised questions about the UCI's behavior in the Brochard case with the revelation that the UCI had accepted a pre-dated medical certificate in violation of its own rules."

Judge Daniel Delegove told the court, "Monsieur Brochard, you were cleared by a forged document." Brochard did not lose his world title, however, as the offense had taken place more than three years previously.

After his suspension was lifted, Brochard came back and won a stage of the Vuelta a España a couple of months afterward. He left the Festina team at the end of the season; for the 2000 season, he signed with the French team Jean Delatour. The Festina team would continue until 2001, but the name of the watch manufacturer would become better known for the scandal that emerged during the 1998

Tour de France than for any results Festina cyclists achieved.

Brochard continued racing until 2008, notching up a multitude of wins for various French teams. Since he retired, he has continued to cycle, competing in events like the 24 Hours of Le Mans, while some of his teammates such as Richard Virenque have gone on to successful media careers.

When Brochard was asked about the events later, and his admission of guilt, he would say, "It was ultimately beneficial, even liberating. If there was the same collective will to speak out now, perhaps there would be less suspicion. Of course, it was a bad story, but these days I am positive. I look for the positive angle in everything."

At the time, it seemed that Brochard had gotten away lightly, with only a six-month ban and a successful return to the peloton. Still, alongside other members of the Festina team, his name will always be synonymous with one of the biggest drug stories to hit the sport.

12

Another Drug Scandal

A few months into the 2004 season, after winning the world title in Canada the previous year, the Spanish cyclist Igor Astarloa was asked by a journalist if he felt there was any truth behind the supposed curse of the rainbow jersey. Astarloa replied, "No, I don't believe that. But I still haven't won a race this season; I ended up second two times and both these times [Paolo] Bettini was first. But, well I'm not superstitious. I think it was essential to win the World Championship and from then on, who knows? But I don't think it's bad luck." Two days later, he was involved in a car crash in Italy.

Astarloa was in the passenger seat when the car he was traveling in was struck by another vehicle. He suffered head injuries and experienced some pain and nausea. He was sent to the nearest hospital in Brescia, where he was fitted with a neck brace. He would miss the following weekend's Critérium International.

Although it was an unfortunate accident, it would hardly have been deemed to be enough of a setback for the season to be considered "cursed." Regrettably for the Spaniard, worse was to come.

Despite his denial of any belief in the curse, a cycling journalist in an interview prior to the 2004 season did note that Astarloa did have one peculiar superstition, which he had picked up from his time in Italy. During the interview, each time the Basque rider was asked about particular cycling accidents that had occurred during his career, he had a tendency to touch his testicles for luck.

The World Championships had returned to Canada in 2003 for the first time since 1974, when they were held in Montreal. This time, Hamilton, Ontario, was the host city. One hundred eighty riders lined up at the start of the race, where they faced twenty-one laps of a twelve-and-a-half-kilometer circuit. The course included two longish drags, which weren't considered too taxing.

The race started under gray skies, but that didn't deter the crowds: An estimated hundred thousand spectators lined the route. Despite having had his best season to date, Astarloa would not have been listed among the favorites for the race. The Basque had won La Flèche Wallonne earlier in the season, in addition to a stage of Volta a la Comunitat Valenciana.

The opening laps were uneventful enough, and the first significant break didn't go until the fifth lap. Dutchman Koos Moerenhout got a gap on the climb up Claremont Access and was out on his own for two laps until Colombian Victor Hugo Peña and Norwegian Bjørnar Vestøl bridged across. When this trio gained a lead of three minutes over the peloton, the Italians went to the front of the bunch to start reeling them in. The leaders did gain some impetus when Swiss rider Fabian Cancellara got across to them with ten laps remaining. However, they only stayed clear for another lap.

With nine laps remaining, it was *gruppo compatto*. A number of other attacks took place, but were pulled back each time. Bettini came to the fore, but even he struggled to break apart the race.

On the nineteenth lap, Astarloa suffered some misfortune when he crashed on a corner at the top of the climb of Beckett Drive, but he was unhurt. It was not any particular injury he was concerned about, however; as he recounted afterward, "My first real concern was for the bike. I knew I hadn't been badly injured, but it's really complicated to get technical assistance in the Worlds and I had no idea if I would be able to get back on." Fortunately for Astarloa, the bike was okay, and he regained the group pretty easily.

Once again, other attacks went clear and were reeled back each time by the Italians. With just one lap to go, the peloton was still very large. Astarloa's teammate and former World Champion was Óscar Freire still in the bunch, and Astarloa asked him how he was feeling. Freire replied, "I can't follow Bettini. You go ahead."

On the final ascent of Beckett Drive, the Belgian Peter Van Petegem attacked. Astarloa was able to go with him, along with Bettini, former winner from Switzerland Oscar Camenzind, Dutchman Michael Boogerd, and Bo Hamburger of Denmark. They quickly opened up a twenty-five-second gap.

Despite some good work by the US and German teams, they could make few inroads into the leaders' advantage. Then, on the final climb, their lead started to crumble. A number of riders managed to bridge across, including Alejandro Valverde, but as they did so Astarloa made his move.

Bettini tried but was unable to close the gap, and Astarloa, a noted descender, was able to maintain his lead on the run in toward the finish line. Astarloa later described the decisive move: "Jumping where I did, with a long ascent to climb, was a risk too. But having Alejandro Valverde bridge across to the chasing group and act as a brake meant I knew I had a chance. [Note: Astarloa was inferring that the presence of Valverde in their group would make the chasers more reluctant to pursue him.] Plus, the headwind was so strong, which helped enormously: whoever was on somebody's wheel if they tried to get across would have a big advantage over the guy leading and doing the chasing because of the wind. So everybody sat up a bit too long waiting for everyone else."

Astarloa had enough of an advantage over the others to savor the win in the last few hundred meters, and he recounted those moments: "I knew I couldn't be caught so I did enjoy those last couple of hundred meters. I had time to remember how hard it had been to become a pro, to think about my family as well. Wearing the rainbow jersey is something only very few riders have achieved, and for a Classics rider you can't get higher than this."

As he crossed the line to take the win, the sprint started to open for second place. Astarloa's teammate Valverde took the silver medal ahead of Van Petegem and Bettini. Afterward, Astarloa told journalists, "I really can't believe I won today. I just found the right moment to get away and was able to win. I've already won a classic this year but the World Championships, that was just a dream until today. I still can't believe it. Yes, on the last lap I got in the good break. Van Petegem was really strong but I was good too."

Hamburger admitted afterward that Astarloa was the strongest in the break, saying, "We were riding well together in the break, but on the last climb, there was a strong headwind and Astarloa was the only one who had a little bit extra and he won."

Bettini, on the other hand, told reporters, "I just can't accept what happened today and I wanted to win." Spanish TV reported afterward that Bettini had tried to buy the race from Astarloa. "He offered me money in the final but I felt so good and I really wanted to win," said Astarloa. It's one of those strange aspects of the sport that a blind eye is usually turned to what is essentially a bribe. There have been numerous instances down through the years of cyclists buying and selling races, and there are rarely any repercussions for those involved.

Shortly before his World Championship win, Astarloa had signed for the French team Cofidis, and he would not be the only rainbow jersey wearer who would be racing for Cofidis the following season. World Time Trial Champion David Millar was also a member of the team, and Laurent Gané had gained his world title on the track in the sprint. It was a move that Astarloa would undoubtedly go on to rue, as he along with Millar would be implicated in yet another scandal to rock the sport.

Prior to his move to the French team, there were rumors going around about Astarloa. The Cofidis president François Migraine in an interview with *L'Équipe* revealed that the new World Champion had been signed despite the cloud of suspicion hanging over him. "After the Worlds, he was suspected of doping. What am I supposed to do?" Migraine asked. He went on to say that Astarloa was a rider he preferred to sign given his steady progress and apparent hard work. "That for me is satisfying."

The team president confirmed that he would be monitoring the results of his new signing: "Now I'll pay attention to him, and if at the end of the season he has no results, that might tell me something, but honestly I'm inclined to give him my confidence. The UCI said he was clean, so for me he was clean."

At the team's presentation in 2004, it opened with a tribute to the Kazakh cyclist Andrei Kivilev, who had died in a tragic accident in Paris–Nice the previous year, while racing for Cofidis. Afterward Astarloa was interviewed by veteran cycling commentator Daniel Mangeas, and the Basque rider outlined his ambitions for the season. "I'll be training for the Classics and World Championships," he told Mangeas. "It will be difficult, but I'll do my best. I want to win the World Cup."

The Cofidis team manager, Alain Bondue, also outlined his confidence in his new signee's abilities, saying, "It wasn't luck to sign Astarloa. We have been after him for two years."

But the season started to fall apart pretty quickly for Astarloa and the rest of the team. Less than a week after the presentation, a former Cofidis rider, Marek Rutkiewicz, was arrested at Charles de Gaulle Airport in Paris. This began a police investigation into the Cofidis team that would see other riders such as Philippe Gaumont, Robert Sassone, and Cédric Vasseur arrested and questioned shortly afterward.

The team's headquarters in Amiens was searched, and medical

files were seized. Initially, David Millar denied any knowledge of drug use within the team, saying, "All I can say is it's not a Cofidis problem and it's certainly got nothing to do with me. It's a scandal involving Madejak, not a collective conspiracy." The man he was speaking of was Boguslaw Madejak, a soigneur with the team, who was said to have supplied Rutkiewicz with EPO.

However, Millar was also arrested and questioned by police. During a search of his apartment, they found empty vials of Eprex, a brand of EPO, as well as used syringes. The Scot was charged and found guilty of doping, and banned from the sport for two years. Because Astarloa had just joined the team, he wasn't suspected of having any involvement in the emerging scandal.

Cofidis initially declared that there was no systematic doping program within the team, and that individual riders had made their own personal decisions to dope. However, Millar would later contradict this, telling the BBC, "I had grown up with the team. They were my home away from home. I had gone through the ranks of the team very quickly. They twisted my mentality. You convince yourself that is what you have to do. I was getting paid a lot of money; there were seventy people working for the team and I was the figurehead. They treated me in a way that said 'if you don't do this then you are putting all our jobs at risk, we need you to be performing at your best.'"

The team announced that it was suspending its racing program just prior to Paris–Roubaix. When news of the team suspension emerged, Astarloa requested that Cofidis tear up his contract, to

Bettini

Igor Astarloa in one of his rare appearances for Cofidis.
He left after the team suspended its racing program following
revelations of doping by its riders.

allow him to join a new team. It subsequently made a statement
noting that "the World Champion has been released on his request
from his contract with Cofidis. He is now free to sign for another
team and to take part in the races for which he prepared especially."

Astarloa made the move back to Italy, signing for Lampre for the remainder of the season. His performances were underwhelming, however. Apart from a win in a criterium in Holland, his only performance of note was a stage win in the Brixia Tour. He parted ways with Lampre at the end of the year and signed with his old manager from Saeco, Claudio Corti. The former World Champion was confident that he could make amends for his disastrous year in the rainbow jersey, telling journalists, "I think I'm physically back to my best and I'm confident of doing well this year. The spirit in the new team is what I need to help me be successful again."

He had limited success with Corti's new team Barloworld, however, and would win just a stage of the Tour of Burgos and Milan–Turin during his two years with the team. He never regained the form he had shown in 2003, and drifted from team to team. He would end up being released by Milram in 2008 for irregular blood readings; his subsequent team Amica Chips folded for financial reasons the following year. He finally retired after he was announced as being one of the first few riders with suspicious blood values found through the UCI's biological passport testing program.

He subsequently spoke to the Spanish newspaper *El Mundo Deportivo* about the doping suspicions hanging over him: "Simply because someone suspects you, they eliminate you from cycling. I have been racing bikes for 22 years. All that you've done in your life is finished because of suspicion. You don't need to have tested positive. I see all too well that things aren't fair at all. It's better to leave this bad environment and find a better place to be. I've never tested positive, I've kept racing and I'm not even sanctioned."

Astarloa was joining the list of cyclists who would use the "I never tested positive" line without actually denying that they had doped. It seems to be a way for some cyclists to justify their own actions: They believe that if they weren't caught, then they didn't cheat.

Astarloa went on to say, "Cycling isn't the same as when I started. We used to really enjoy ourselves; there was a good atmosphere between everyone. Having spent 10 years as a professional and seen the before and the now, where you are always under suspicion and there are all kinds of bad affairs, I'm bowing out voluntarily."

David Millar, his fellow rainbow jersey wearer from Cofidis, returned to the sport after his two-year ban and became an advocate for a cleaner sport. Astarloa, however, despite having been exonerated from any blame in the Cofidis scandal—and also having retired from the sport—was given a two-year suspension by the Spanish Cycling Federation's Disciplinary Commission as well as a thirty-five-thousand-euro fine, due to the findings of the biological passport program. Astarloa, it appeared had joined the list of other World Championship winners whose downfall in the sport had started as soon as he took the title.

13

Double Tragedy

Although the stories in this book are primarily about the World Champions who won their titles on the road, it would be difficult to broach the subject of the curse of the rainbow jersey without recalling the story of Isaac Gálvez. Unlike other wearers of the jersey, Gálvez won his title on the track. The fate that befell him is not only one of the most tragic accidents involving a rainbow jersey wearer, but also happens to be one of the saddest tales in a sport beset by misfortune.

Isaac Gálvez López was born in 1975 in Vilanova i la Geltrú, near Barcelona, to a cycling-mad family. He inherited his passion for the sport from his father; his younger sister Débora would also go on to be very successful at cycling. Débora excelled at time trialing, and would go on to win national titles at both junior and senior level.

Isaac first showed promise on the track. He had taken his first rainbow jersey in 1999 in the Madison event in Berlin. The Madison is a team event with two members on each team; one of those two must be racing at all times. When the second rider takes over, he usually receives a hand sling from his partner to launch him into the race. The event was first run in Madison Square Garden, hence the name. Gálvez's partner in the event was Joan Llaneras, a more experienced rider from Majorca.

Following on from Gálvez's triumph on the track, he was offered a professional contract with Kelme. It didn't take him long to adapt to the paid ranks: He took a win in his opening season in Clásica de Almería, and he proved to be a consistent winner thereafter. He took victories in the Tours of Catalonia and Majorca and the Critérium International, among other races, in the following seasons.

He developed exceptional bike-handling skills on the track, which he would put to good use on the road. In fact, he was known for being able to "bunny-hop" his track bike from the boards up onto a chair and balance upon it before hopping the bike back down to the track.

In 2004, he transferred to the Îles Baléars team, where he continued to add to his palmarès. His most successful season to date was 2006, with wins in the Trofeo Mallorca, Trofeo Alcúdia, and a stage win in the Four Days of Dunkirk in addition to repeating his 1999 victory with Llaneras in the World Madison Championship.

His good form was recognized by the team, as he was selected for that year's Tour de France. He rode well in the race, and came close to nabbing a win—he was second on one stage and sixth on another. His family and girlfriend Davinia turned up at the race to show their support.

Toward the end of the season Gálvez was contracted, alongside Llaneras, to take part in a number of races on the lucrative six-day circuit. The duo came close to winning one of the first races that winter, finishing in second place in Amsterdam. Their next race was in Munich, where another good performance saw them finishing in sixth. Despite his busy schedule, he still managed to find time to marry Davinia after the Munich Six-Day. Unfortunately the couple didn't have much time to spend together, as Isaac had to return to Northern Europe to compete in his next race, the Ghent Six-Day.

The Ghent Six-Day is one of the most anticipated events on the calendar, with many tickets selling out months in advance. Spectators look forward to nights of loud music, not to mention excesses of beer and fries. Gálvez was teaming with his Madison partner, Joan Llaneras, for the event. The track at the Kuipke velodrome was a mere 167 meters long, which made for exciting racing on its fifty-five-degree banking. Because each lap is so short, however, the race can sometimes be confusing for spectators.

Cor Vos

Isaac Gálvez with his Madison partner, Joan Llaneras.

On the Wednesday evening, Gálvez had a minor crash, but he laughed it off afterward. Both he and Llaneras told a Belgian reporter that crashes were part of track racing, although the duo did complain that they didn't like the track in Ghent due to its shortness. The pair rode well, winning a number of the races over the first few nights. After day four, they lay in third position overall.

The fifth night saw another packed house, but it was on this second-to-last night—with Gálvez and Llaneras in second place overall—that the tragedy unfolded. During the last Madison of the night, the Spaniard collided with Dimitri De Fauw when they were racing at over fifty kilometers per hour, and he flew toward the track wall. Such was the impact that he was lifted off his bike and hit the railing at the top of the wall. Gálvez then fell back onto the track and slid to the flat area at the bottom.

Journalist Les Woodland witnessed the accident. "Gálvez had blood on his lips," he recounted, "and what I learned later, was that on falling back to the track he had caught his chin on the metal fence and bitten his tongue. He appeared to signal something, lifting one hand, then fell still. That was when his soigneur began pumping his heart. First-aid people set to work. And then a place which moments before had throbbed to cheers, music, commentary and the laughter of people conga-dancing with plastic beer glasses in their hands fell again to a murmur."

De Fauw described the crash afterward. "I sat maybe in fourth or fifth position in the field," he explained. "Iljo Keisse had just attacked. We came out of the bend onto the finish straight when there was a wave in the peloton. I saw nothing. I heard nothing, but suddenly there was Isaac, who started to chase Iljo behind me. I didn't see him coming. We hooked our handlebars together and were thrown to the top of the track. It all happened in the fraction of a second."

De Fauw also crashed and initially seemed to come off badly, but he was eventually able to get to his feet and make his way toward his cabin in the center of the track.

The medics were quickly on the scene and were able to resuscitate Gálvez briefly at the track. However, there was a delay of ten minutes before an ambulance arrived. The race organizer, Patrick Sercu, realizing the seriousness of the accident, pushed away a photographer taking shots of the scene.

Joan Llaneras made a phone call from the velodrome to Davinia Gálvez, informing her that there had been a serious accident involving her new husband. The entire crowd now knew that the situation was a lot more critical than first thought. Medics continued to try to get his heart working again even as he was being wheeled toward the ambulance. There were heartbreaking scenes as a clearly distraught Joan Llaneras ran behind his friend; a number of spectators actually fainted from the shock of what they were witnessing.

Despite the best efforts of the medics, Gálvez died on the way to the University Hospital in Ghent. He was pronounced dead at approximately one thirty on Sunday morning. His death had been caused by massive internal bleeding after the impact ruptured several ribs, which were pushed against his heart.

When the race organizers learned of the tragic news, the race was canceled. Announcer Rob Discart was visibly emotional as he told the crowd that the race was over "out of respect to Gálvez, his family and the other riders." Another member of the organizing team had to be taken to the hospital with chest pains.

Despite his lack of serious physical injuries, De Fauw was also taken to the hospital suffering from shock when he realized the extent of Gálvez's injuries. De Fauw was treated at the same hospital as Gálvez, where he learned the devastating news when he overheard two doctors talking about "that rider who died in the bike race."

As De Fauw was being treated at the hospital, Iljo Keisse and Robert Bartko were officially declared the winners, but Keisse took absolutely no satisfaction from this. "We are on the palmarès, that's all," he said afterward. "It means absolutely nothing. My dream became a nightmare. No, this edition has no winners, only losers."

Iljo's father, Ronnie, ran a bar named De Karper near to the velodrome, and heard the news of the crash on the radio that night. His bar was packed with regulars who were looking forward to Iljo's victory. Upon hearing the news, however, Ronnie realized how serious the crash was, turned off the music, stopped serving, and asked his customers to leave. "It was no time to be happy when a man's life was in danger," he said.

One man who was racked with guilt over the death of Gálvez was Dimitri De Fauw. When the Belgian spoke to the press after the accident, the twenty-five-year-old told them, "I will carry this with me for the rest of my life. Only time can heal my wounds." He returned to the velodrome a number of times in the days immediately afterward, but he was really struggling to come to terms with what had happened. "I haven't touched the bike since Saturday." De Fauw said that the first time he tried to go back to the track, he collapsed, and the second time he could stay only ten minutes. "The last time I laid flowers at the place where they tried to resuscitate Gálvez. Now I no longer want to see the building."

Six-day racing started in the 1870s. It was extremely dangerous during its first few decades, with many deaths occurring on the tracks of Europe and North America. However, Gálvez's death had been the first since 1964, when Louis de Vos had died in a race in Montreal.

Eddy Merckx had spoken to Gálvez during the event, and recalled afterward, "I was in the Kuipke on Wednesday and had a short conversation with the World Champion. To learn in the morning that this boy died comes very hard. A rider can fall ten times without a lot happening. This must be very hard on his family and friends."

Around two thousand people attended his funeral, including fellow cyclists such as Alejandro Valverde, Óscar Pereiro, and Miguel Poblet. Gálvez was interred in his place of birth, Vilanova i la Geltrú. Rob Discart also attended from Ghent, and said of Davinia, Isaac's widow, "She was completely shocked and had to be supported; that was a heartrending scene. Everybody who was here had a hard time."

The following spring, riders competing in the Vuelta a Murcia donated their winnings to Gálvez's widow. A plaque honoring the Spaniard was revealed at the Kuipke at the following year's Ghent Six-Day, which was attended by both Davinia and Joan Llaneras.

Llaneras had contemplated retiring after the misfortune, but eventually did return to the sport. He told the Spanish newspaper *Marca*, "Clearly I thought about leaving it all. It was the first reaction. Logical. Natural. Normal after what had happened, but life goes on, and giving it all up, unfortunately, will not solve anything. In addition, the track is my life, is my dream, my family, it is almost everything to me."

Llaneras went on to win a silver medal in the Madison at the Beijing Olympics, and it's conceivable to think that Isaac Gálvez could have joined him in winning that medal. He retired from the sport not long afterward.

The organizers of the Six-Day were later cleared by Jean Soenen, the public prosecutor of Ghent, of any negligence. Soenen stated that they had no responsibility for Gálvez's death; he felt that they had taken all the necessary safety measures. He also commented on the fact that Gálvez's bicycle showed no sign of any mechanical failure.

Another World Madison Champion had also been involved in a serious track accident a number of years previously. The 1998 World Champion, Matthew Gilmore, was competing in the Herning Six-Day when he collided with a mechanic who was standing trackside. He was unconscious for ten minutes, and onlookers feared the worst. Despite suffering serious injuries including broken ribs, facial injuries, and a collapsed lung, however, Gilmore would make a full recovery and go on to compete at the highest level again.

Unfortunately, the death of Gálvez was not the final tragedy associated with the events in Ghent. Dimitri De Fauw continued to struggle with guilt; he had a lot of difficulty in coming to terms with what had happened that night. He even gave up the bike for a short time. He spoke about his turmoil shortly afterward: "I have had some painful and very emotional days and nights. The idea of hanging up the bike hasn't occurred to me. What good will that do? It is no solution to stop. In fact, this accident must be an extra incentive for me to go further with racing. However, right now I am not ready for that. I would like to thank my team for giving me the time to complete this process in my own way."

De Fauw did make a comeback, but his career was on the decline and he moved from one small Belgian team to another. The Belgian newspaper *Het Laatse Nieuws* printed allegations from an unnamed former Quick Step rider about systematic doping within the team, and the rumors doing the rounds were that De Fauw was the whistleblower. De Fauw's mother would later accuse journalists of twisting her son's words, after they had coaxed him into an interview in the months following Gálvez's death in a bid to try to discredit his former manager at Quick Step, Patrick Lefévère. His uncle Mark De Fauw said that his nephew had been taken advantage of at a time when he was still feeling the effects of Gálvez's death.

"He was angry when he read the newspaper article," said De Fauw's mother, Claudine Verhoeven. "'I did not say that at all!' [he said], they had totally distorted his words." These problems did not rest easy in his already troubled mind.

In the winter of 2009, De Fauw had raced at the Grenoble Six-Day. He returned to Belgium afterward with another rider who ridden on the track in Ghent on that fateful night, Iljo Keisse. On the track, all had seemed well with De Fauw. He entertained the crowd, thumping his chest like Tarzan when he took a victory. However, off the track, he barely spoke to any of the other riders.

Keisse did not recall anything unusual in his compatriot's demeanor on the overnight drive back to Belgium, recalling, "I dropped De Fauw off at his home in Ghent at 8 AM and we still laughed together. I did not find him any different from usual. 'I'll call you to go training,' he told me."

De Fauw never did call his friend to go training. Later that day, he took his own life. Despite being told numerous times by friends, as well as those who witnessed the crash in Ghent, that he was not to blame for Gálvez's death, he could not get over the tragic events that night. Keisse wished his friend had looked for help, saying afterward, "If only 'Dimi' had ever used the word *depression* or seen Gálvez's death for what it was, an accident, or realized that the *Het Laatse Nieuws* thing was bigger in his own mind than anyone else's."

It seemed that De Fauw eventually reasoned that he could not go on carrying the guilt from the accident. He was only twenty-eight.

14

Death of a Brother

Despite their many differences, the two great Italian cyclists of the postwar era, Fausto Coppi and Gino Bartali, shared a common bond. Both of them had lost brothers to crashes in races. Coppi's brother Serse died in the Giro del Piemonte in 1951, while Bartali's brother Giulio died in a race in 1936. Decades later, the brother of another top Italian cyclist would die in a tragic accident, and the circumstances that surrounded it would make it all the more heartbreaking.

In 2000, Paolo Bettini emerged as arguably the best one-day rider in the world. After winning Liège–Bastogne–Liège that year, the diminutive rider, nicknamed "The Cricket" or "Il Grillo" went on to claim wins over the next few years in the Giro di Lombardia, the Clásica San Sebastián, Milan–San Remo, and the Olympics, among other races. However, one race eluded him: the World Championships. This was despite the fact that it was more often than not held on a course that would suit his abilities. He had been a professional since 1997, and it seemed that he might join the list of great riders never to have taken the world title.

Il Grillo had gotten into cycling at a young age through his brother Sauro, who was six years older. Paolo used to travel with his parents, Giuliano and Giuliana, to watch him compete all over Tuscany. "I grew up going to watch my brother Sauro race with my parents and when Sauro stopped racing I was nine and I automatically took his place." His father helped him build his first bike, using parts salvaged from various other machines. He then painted the frame orange.

Some considered Sauro the more talented of the brothers. "Sauro was the better climber of the two," Giuliano said. "But he didn't have the character and the willpower of his younger brother. Sauro sometimes liked to go to the beach, or to go fishing, instead of training. Paolo didn't, you never had to encourage him to train, he automatically did so."

The training paid off: Bettini won twenty-three out of the first twenty-four races he entered. He remained focused throughout his teenage years, and he would go on to clinch a professional contract after finishing fourth in the 1996 U-23 World Championships.

He was signed by the MG-Technogym team, where he worked as a domestique for Michele Bartoli for a number of years. As the latter's strength faded, and Bettini was coming more to the fore, it seemed inevitable that the two would clash. Matters came to a head at the World Championships in 2001 in Lisbon, where the younger man finished in second place behind Óscar Freire. Bettini had refused to lead out Bartoli in the sprint, because he felt he had a better chance himself. They would race on different teams the following season.

In 2005, Bettini came close again to capturing the world title. He had been one of the most aggressive riders in Madrid and was part of the small leading group with just one kilometer to go. However, they were caught by a chase group, and it was Bettini's trade teammate Tom Boonen who won the sprint to take the title. Il Grillo had also been a member of the Italian team who had worked so well together to help Mario Cipollini to take the win back in 2002 in Zolder. It was the last time that an Italian had won the World Championships.

One of the main objectives Bettini set himself for the 2006 season was to capture the world title, and he had shown consistent form throughout the season, winning the Italian Championships as well as stages in the Giro and the Vuelta. His performance in the Vuelta suggested that he was coming into form at just the right time.

The World Championships were being held in Austria that year, in Mozart's home city of Salzburg. The lap that the riders faced was considerably longer than normal at twenty-two kilometers, so they would only have twelve circuits to make. Despite there being two climbs per lap, many felt that the lap wasn't difficult enough, and that the race would come down once again to a sprint finish.

As is usually the case in the World Championships, an early break went clear, which contained two Italians, Matteo Tosatto and Rinaldo Nocentini, among others. Bettini meanwhile maintained a low profile, staying in the middle of the peloton for the first few laps. The break gained a massive lead of fifteen minutes during the fifth lap, but this was as good as it got for them. It was then that a number of teams started to work together to bring them back.

With forty kilometers remaining, the early leaders were caught.

A number of counterattacks then went clear, including an attempt by Bettini with the German Fabian Wegmann, but they were soon caught. Others also tried and failed. It seemed that the predictions of a bunch sprint may have been right.

On the final climb of the Gschaiderberg, Luca Paolini gave Bettini a fast lead out, which enabled him to get a gap. On the descent, however, he was caught by the peloton, which still numbered about forty riders. Despite more attempts, nobody could get clear of the bunch.

Coming into the last kilometer, it seemed that the race was destined to be won by one of the strong sprinters, such as the Belgian Tom Boonen or Australian Robbie McEwen. The Spaniards Samuel Sánchez and Alejandro Valverde led the way through the corner after the red kite, with German Erik Zabel behind them and then Bettini. They took a risk going around that corner that the others in the race wouldn't. This move gained the quartet a gap of a few meters on the rest of the group as they went under the bridge. Sanchez kept the pace high at the front until the 250-meters-to-go marker. However, Valverde was unable to make the most of this lead-out, as Zabel opened his sprint. It looked like the German could take the title, but in the last few meters Bettini came past for the win.

When he crossed the line, he was greeted by his wife Monica, his daughter Veronica, and his parents. His brother Sauro, meanwhile, had organized a barbecue back in their home town of La California for his supporters' club.

After crossing the line, Bettini told reporters that "the last corner was the determining factor, as we four managed to create the gap just there. I dedicate this victory to everyone who trusted my abilities, who believed that I could win—it feels incredible! What can I say?"

"I still don't know how I ended up in that position," he revealed later. "Instinctively, I just saw something brewing at the front of the bunch. I'd been on Boonen's wheel for a kilometer or so and I looked left and saw Sanchez giving Valverde a signal. From there, I don't know what happened. I don't know how or why but my instinct told me to go for it. If I tried to do the same thing again, I'm sure that 99 times out of 100 I'd end up on the tarmac, but for some reason, that time I made it."

His win was attributed by some to his tactical nous as much as his strength on the bike. "Bettini won the world title with a flash of inspiration," Italian team manager Franco Ballerini said afterward. "Paolo is a genius in the decisive moments of a race like that because he has the ability to understand what is going to happen and like a great chess player he anticipates his rivals' moves."

Bettini said afterward, "I feel like I've completed my career now I've won the rainbow jersey. I've won everything I can. OK, there is still the Tour of Flanders, but I'm satisfied with my career now. I'm very proud that I can wear the rainbow jersey for a year and proud that it was another perfect performance from the Italian team."

It could have been a difficult World Championships for the Italians, as the team included not only Bettini, but also Danilo Di Luca, Filippo Pozzato, and Davide Rebellin. However, it was an indication of the strength of Franco Ballerini's man-management skills that he was able to persuade all of them to work for Bettini.

Unfortunately, just ten days after his Worlds win, Bettini's world was turned upside down. Sauro was involved in a traffic accident in Bibbona, not far from his home. He had been attending a meeting that evening regarding the organization of an upcoming party to celebrate his brother's Worlds win. At around half past eleven on his way home, he overturned his gold Subaru after hitting a concrete post. The car left the road through a guardrail and ended up in a ditch.

Help arrived quickly and Sauro was rushed to hospital, but it was too late. He was pronounced dead shortly after his arrival. He left behind a wife and ten-year-old son, Francesco.

Paolo was away racing at the time he received the news. His Quick Step team withdrew from the Coppa Sabatini race later in the week upon hearing of the death. It was a race Bettini had won previously. Sauro's funeral was held later that week in their parish church of California-Bibbona.

Paolo was devastated; he felt that he couldn't cope with continuing in the sport. He wanted to retire, but his parents tried to dissuade him. Giuliano and Giuliana said that continuing to race was a way of honoring his brother's memory, and that it is what Sauro would have wanted.

Paolo would tell the Italian cycling magazine *Bicisport* afterward about that difficult time: "When Sauro was killed it was like a bolt of lightning, and I realized that cycling and even winning the world title was worth very little in comparison to losing a brother. I decided to quit after Sauro's death because there didn't seem any point and I didn't have the strength to do it."

Paolo would eventually continue in the sport. The next big race on the calendar for Bettini was the Tour of Lombardy, and he was determined to do a good ride in memory of his brother. He had won the race the previous year, and could normally be counted as one of the favorites. Nobody knew, though, what frame of mind Paolo was in after such a traumatic time.

The race started over the Swiss border in Mendrisio that year, with the finish in Como. As with the Worlds, Bettini maintained a low profile, staying in the middle of the peloton for much of the race, unsure whether he would bow out or push on. It was on the legendary climb of the Ghisallo where his aggression came through.

After passing the famous chapel at the top of the Ghisallo, Bettini went clear with Fränk Schleck, Davide Rebellin, and Danilo Di Luca, among others. The lead group was whittled down to just twelve men. Bettini then followed an attack by Di Luca before going clear alone. Only the German Fabian Wegmann was able to bridge across to the flying Bettini. On the final climb, though, he dropped Wegmann to descend alone to the finish.

As he crossed the line, Bettini was in floods of tears. He pointed to the sky to remember his brother. His family was there to greet him, including Sauro's son, Francesco. Paolo had persuaded his nephew to come to the race, as he had hoped that he could pull off a victory in memory of his brother and Francesco's father.

"I wasn't riding on my own," Bettini said afterward. "While I was on the attack I could feel that Sauro was with me. I've won a lot of races and many of them have been special, but this is the best one thanks to my determination and with some help from someone. I've got to look forward in life. You can't change things in the past but you can in the future."

Paolo Bettini crossing the line to win the Giro di Lombardia just days after his brother had been killed in an accident.

His win in Lombardy echoed what Gino Bartali had achieved all those years previously when his brother had died. Bartali also had made the decision to quit cycling, until his sister convinced him to start again. He came back to win the Tour of Lombardy, which he dedicated to his older brother Giulio.

Bettini described his victory in Lombardy as the most beautiful win of his career. "It's just untouchable for what it represents," he said. "A week earlier, I'd seriously wanted to give up. Sauro was the reason I started cycling, and with him gone there didn't seem any point in carrying on. My parents and family convinced me to carry on and they inspired me to win Lombardy for Sauro."

Despite his win in Lombardy, the personal tragedy seemed to deeply affect Bettini's performances. He had limited success in the 2007 season, with just a stage win in both the Tour of California and the Vuelta. However, toward the end of the season, Bettini retained his world title in Stuttgart, the first rider to do so since Gianni Bugno in 1992, and only the fifth rider ever to achieve the feat.

Bettini retired from the peloton in 2008. After his brother died, he seemed to lose some of his enthusiasm for the sport. His family became even more important to him, and he didn't like spending too much time away from them. Even his zest for training had seemed to wane. He revealed how much the death of his brother meant to him when he would later say, "I don't know what happiness is now. It's hard for me to be really happy about anything now. I just want the people close to me to be okay. That's my idea of happiness."

Unfortunately, he was struck by personal tragedy again in 2010.

His friend and the man who helped to guide him to his two World Championships wins was killed in a car crash. Franco Ballerini had been taking part in a rally in Larciano in Tuscany when their car left the road during one of the stages. Ballerini was taken to the hospital, but later died of his injuries. Bettini was devastated, saying, "I lost a great friend, a brother." He would later follow in the footsteps of Ballerini as Italian team manager. He would say, however, "I'd prefer not to have ended up coming into this job the way I did. Franco was close to me when my brother died in 2006, and he made me understand that life goes on."

Tragedy nearly struck the Bettini family again in 2011, when Paolo was involved in a light aircraft crash. He had been a passenger in a plane being flown over the Tyrrhenian Sea by a friend when he had to ditch the aircraft in the sea, near the town of Piombino. Bettini and his friend were able to clamber out of the plane and swim away. They were picked up by a nearby fishing boat, and he escaped with just a small leg injury.

Bettini enjoyed a remarkable career, eclipsing some of the greats of the sport with his number of one-day wins. However, his win in the 2006 Tour of Lombardy and tribute to his brother must stand out as one of the most emotional victories ever seen in cycling. There hasn't been any other World Champion who has been affected by real tragedy so soon after taking the title.

15

The Other Victims

Since the very first World Championships in 1927, dozens of riders have taken the title. I have included stories of just a few of those who were said to have been victims of the curse, but there have been others. They may not have been as high-profile as some of the cyclists, or their misfortune or fall from grace as obvious, but the curse has still been mentioned when discussing their year in the rainbow colors.

One of the first riders who is sometimes cited as being a victim of the curse is the 1958 World Champion, Ercole Baldini. The Fast Train from Forli, as he was nicknamed, won his title in Rheims, after winning the Giro d'Italia earlier in the year, and he was still only twenty-five years old. He was subsequently offered a large salary to move to the Ignis team. The following season, he didn't justify his large salary—he notched up just five wins after taking sixteen the previous season. His biggest win was a stage in the Tour de France. Fans started to jeer the World Champion, and cartoons started appearing in cycling magazines depicting him as an overweight mercenary, struggling up mountains while weighed down by a bag of gold.

It was suggested that Baldini had become lazy after switching teams, and that he didn't train hard enough, but he refuted those claims. "People think that it is the money that stops me training properly, but I train as hard as I ever have, and I haven't altered my methods."

When questioned about his weight at the time, he explained, "I had to have many lay-offs, including one that necessitated a tricky operation on my leg and during them I put on weight. I would then have to fight twice as hard to get rid of it, so I was constantly going into races tired. It just became a vicious circle."

The following year was even worse for Baldini, who won just once. He subsequently retired at the end of 1964, never having lived up to his potential. Years later, Baldini would reveal that he did in fact live the good life after winning the Worlds. "I did develop a love of good food and I'd eat enough for two," he said. "I'd even hide extra nibbles in my room. After training I'd always head straight for the kitchen before taking a shower or a rest." So it appeared that despite his initial denials, the title and subsequent huge contract did impact his dedication to the sport.

Eddy Merckx is just one of four riders to have won the title three times, and obviously the more often a rider wins, the higher the like-lihood is that he will have a difficult subsequent season. Having won in Heerlen in 1967, and Mendrisio in 1971, Merckx took his final title in Montreal in 1974. The following year, he was leading the Tour de France, and it seemed that he might go on to become the first rider to win the Tour six times. However, on the fourteenth stage to the summit of the volcano, the Puy de Dôme, a spectator emerged from the crowd and punched Merckx in the kidneys. He struggled afterward and had to be prescribed medication. He crashed a few days later and fractured his jaw. Remarkably enough, he went on to finish the race in second place. That punch was the start of the slide for Merckx, and his dominance was over. He wouldn't win the Tour or the Worlds again, and had limited success thereafter.

The controversial Worlds of 1988 was referred to earlier, and the unlikely winner from that year, Maurizio Fondriest, had an underwhelming following season. He had just a handful of wins, the highlight being victory in the Coppa Sabatini. However, he was only twenty-four when he wore the rainbow jersey, with his best years still ahead of him. It was less a case of having bad luck than of him not having matured into the rider that he would ultimately become. He went on to win races such as Milan–San Remo and La Flèche Wallonne.

Greg Lemond won the World Championships for the second time in his career in 1989 in Chambéry, having already taken the title back in 1983. He would go on to win the 1986 Tour de France, and it seemed that he could go on to dominate the race for years to come. Then he was accidentally shot in 1987 by his brother-in-law, nearly killing him. His career appeared to be over.

However, Lemond eventually made a comeback to win the closest-ever Tour de France in 1989. Earlier that season, when he had been really struggling, he had told his wife that he would be retiring after the Tour. Following his win on the Champs-Élysées, he decided to aim for the Worlds.

At the end of the rain-sodden race in the Alps, he outsprinted

Dimitri Konyshev and Sean Kelly for the win. Later that year, he was named *Sports Illustrated*'s 1989 Sportsman of the Year. He was the first cyclist to receive the honor, from a magazine that had developed its own reputation for being jinxed (more on which later). Between wearing the rainbow jersey and receiving the *Sports Illustrated* award, it seemed that he was destined to suffer bad luck the following season.

So it came to pass the following spring, when he was diagnosed with mononucleosis. This weakened his immune system and left the American fatigued. His classics campaign was written off. It's very difficult to say that he was a victim of either curse, though, as he did come back in the summer to win the Tour for the third time in his career.

Another American winner of the title, Lance Armstrong, would also go on to have a less-than-stellar subsequent season after winning in Oslo in 1993. Prior to the Worlds, he had taken his first stage win in the Tour de France, in addition to winning the US Championships as part of a triple crown of Stateside races. It would later emerge that Armstrong had helped to ensure he won the three races in the United States by paying off other teams.

In 1994, he didn't have any wins in Europe. His subsequent fall from grace, when he was stripped of all of his Tour de France titles, would also put a question mark over his wins from these earlier years of his career, as it was said that he had actually started doping during his time with the Motorola team. Toward the end of 2012, Armstrong would finally admit to using performance-enhancing drugs

Graham Watson

The 1993 World Champion, Lance Armstrong, has had
the biggest fall from grace of all the title holders.

during his career, and nearly twenty years after taking the rainbow
jersey his downfall was complete. His tale may not have been as
tragic as those of other World Champions, but he was easily the
highest-profile rainbow jersey wearer to suffer a downturn in fortune—albeit of his own making, and many years after the win.

Having won the Worlds for a second time in 1992 in Benidorm,
Gianni Bugno went on to have a forgettable year by his standards the
following season, winning just a handful of smaller races. He had
finished in seventh, second, and third places in the Tour de France

in previous seasons, but after his second Worlds win, he was never a genuine contender again. There was no particular incident or illness—just a slide in form.

Another rider who had a poor season was the 1996 champion, Belgian Johan Museeuw. His reign in the rainbow colors would coincide with an underwhelming spring classics campaign. It would be the first time in a number of seasons that he didn't win any of the big one-day races. Museeuw would also later to confess to the use of performance-enhancing drugs during his career.

As with Ercole Baldini, various other World Champions have been accused of becoming lazy following their win in the Worlds, and resting on their laurels. After winning the Worlds in 2000 in Plouay, the Latvian Romans Vainsteins was signed by Patrick Lefévère for his Domo-Farm Frites team. However, he only won three races while wearing the rainbow bands. He raced for three more seasons after that, winning only one more race. Vainsteins was said to have lacked discipline, which was the reason given for his being sacked from one of his teams. He was also said to have struggled with a number of injuries and with his weight.

In 2004, Óscar Freire joined Alfredo Binda, Rik Van Steenbergen, and Eddy Merckx as the only cyclists to ever win the World Championships three times. However, the Spaniard's career has been affected by numerous injuries, including saddle sores, and back and neck problems. Still, despite his difficulties it's interesting to note that each time he has won the World Championships, Freire has gone on to have a more successful subsequent season.

More recently, Alessandro Ballan won the World Championships in 2008 in Varese. With a kilometer and a half remaining, he unleashed an attack nobody else could follow, and he hung on to win by three seconds. Unfortunately, the following spring he was diagnosed with cytomegalovirus, which sidelined him for months. Later in the year, he was suspended by his team, BMC, as he was one of the riders being questioned in the Mantova investigation. He would suffer further misfortune at the end of 2012, when he was involved in a serious crash while training. He spent a week in intensive care, having broken his femur and ruptured his spleen.

Sometimes there are valid reasons why World Champions don't have prolific subsequent seasons. The 1985 champion, Dutchman Joop Zoetemelk, won just a handful of criteriums during his tenure, but it should be remembered that at thirty-eight he was the oldest winner of the title. It's reasonable to expect that somebody in the twilight of his career will have limited success.

It would be unfair to just dwell on those who had difficult seasons in the rainbow colors, as many cyclists have gone on to have very successful reigns, including Bernard Hinault. The Badger won the title in 1980, and the following year would go on to win the Tour de France, Paris–Roubaix, and Amstel Gold. Cadel Evans, having won the title in 2009, would go on to win La Flèche Wallonne the next year, in addition to wearing both the pink jersey in the Giro and yellow in the Tour de France. Another rider who would have a successful season during his reign was the Belgian Tom Boonen, who won the Tour of Flanders and numerous other races after taking the title.

So it appears at a quick glance that as many cyclists enjoy success during their year in the rainbow jersey as difficulties. However, the successful cyclists are often overlooked—they just don't align well with the hypothesis favored by journalists writing articles on the curse.

16

Spilled Salt and Other Irrational Fears

For centuries, the spilling of salt has been considered by many to bring bad luck. It's also said that you can avert any bad luck from the spillage by throwing more salt over your left shoulder. Some claim the superstition comes from the story that Judas Iscariot spilled salt at the Last Supper. Whatever the background, it's a superstition that many still hold on to today. Some Italian cyclists take it a step farther by not passing salt between each other at meals, but insisting that it be placed on the table instead.

During the 2002 Tour de France, a discussion started one evening around the dinner table of the CSC team about this superstition. The Danish rider Michael Sandstød decided to show his disbelief in it by deliberately spilling salt, and then refusing to throw any over his shoulder. Writer Daniel Coyle reported that Sandstød asked his horrified teammates, "Don't you see? It's just salt."

The following day, on the mountainous stage to La Mongie, Sandstød crashed heavily on a steep descent. He suffered numerous injuries and was admitted to intensive care. For a while, doctors were unsure whether he would pull through, but luckily he recovered.

The story spread quickly around the peloton—not so much about his life-threatening injuries as about the incident with the salt. It gave credence to those who believed in the superstition.

The fear of spilling salt is not the only everyday superstition that has found its way into cycling. The irrational fear of the number 13, or triskaidekaphobia, is also commonly noted during races. Coincidentally, this fear has also been linked by some to the Last Supper, as this was the number of people in attendance. Riders who have been allocated the race number 13 are often seen with it attached upside down. Others go even farther when it comes to their race numbers, and have to follow a particular way of pinning the number on—always pinning from left to right, for instance, then from top to bottom.

Fear of the number 13 results in many riders pinning their number on upside down in races. The World Time Trial Champion Fabian Cancellara follows this tradition.

The former Belgian professional Nico Mattan took his fear of the number 13 to extremes. He said, "Number 13 has a bad ring to me because I heard on a 13th that I wouldn't be able to race anymore because of heart problems. I'm now riding with number 76, if you add 7 and 6, it forms 13; don't even like that really. And I lost the leader's jersey in Paris–Nice on a 13th, so no, I don't like that number."

Mattan's logic increases significantly the total of race numbers he would feel uncomfortable wearing. This thought process and level of superstition must surely weigh on the mind of a cyclist before a race. Fear of the number 13 wasn't the only superstition that the Belgian held on to. One of Mattan's other beliefs can't have been too popular with his teammates: He always wore the same vest under his jersey when he was racing. In addition, he was afraid to walk not only under ladders but also under scaffolding.

Sean Kelly recounted that upon arrival at a hotel, his team's soigneurs would move the Irishman to a different room if they found out that he had been allocated room 13. This wasn't because Kelly was bothered by the number; instead it seemed to put the soigneurs' minds at ease. In the 1993 Tour de France, Belgian rider Peter De Clercq refused to fly on Friday the 13th for a stage transfer. After some discussion, the race director allowed him to use a car instead. Thus he accompanied one of the soigneurs on the arduous 550-kilometer drive from Lac de Madine to Villard-de-Lans. To outsiders, it would seem strange that these riders who would race down vertiginous descents at a hundred kilometers per hour would refuse to fly, despite it being the safest form of transport.

The French cyclist Benoît Poilvet also demonstrated an irrational fear of 13: He would refuse to sleep in hotel rooms or sit on airplane seats that contained the number. Viatcheslav Ekimov was another cyclist who refused to stay in rooms with that number.

The rainbow jersey isn't the only garment in the sport that has been linked to bad luck. Winners of the French Championships are said to suffer from bad luck after donning the blue, white, and red jersey, which they also get to wear for the subsequent year. However, the rainbow jersey curse began to overshadow this myth in the 1980s, and there has been little talk of it since then in the media.

Like other sportspeople, many cyclists carry amulets or good-luck charms with them while they race. Among these was the Dutchman Michael Boogerd, who was supposed to have carried a locket that contained his first tooth, his girlfriend's first tooth, and a four-leaf clover.

Carrying these lucky charms may increase riders' belief that they can perform well. But what happens when the charm goes missing? The German Thomas Ziegler blamed losing a stage of the 2005 Vuelta a España on misplacing his lucky charm, a ring, during the stage. He explained afterward what had happened: "I lost my good-luck charm today. My girlfriend gave me a ring which I always take off my finger during a race—because of the possibility of injuries in a crash—and I wear it on a chain around my neck. But the chain got caught during my breakaway and the ring flew away. Now I have to ride 18 more stages without my good luck charm." So it appears that the use of these amulets can have a negative effect on performances.

A similar incident happened with the American cyclist Tyler Hamilton. Hamilton crashed heavily during the 2003 Tour de France on the very first stage, fracturing his collarbone, but somehow went on to finish the race. Afterward, a friend gave him a vial of salt and a small bottle of water as good-luck charms. Hamilton started racing with the salt in one of his jersey pockets, and taking a small sip of the water before every race thereafter. However, on the first day that he forgot to take the salt with him in the Tour of Holland, he crashed and cracked his femur. He reasoned that the crash was due to forgetting the salt.

Something else that has been seen to affect cyclists negatively are prophecies. Five-time Tour de France winner Jacques Anquetil is probably the cyclist best known for holding on to superstitious beliefs. During the 1964 Tour de France, a fortune-teller called Belline predicted in the newspaper *France-Soir* that the Frenchman would actually die on or around the 13th day of the race.

Anquetil's wife tried to hide the prediction from him, but he found out regardless, and it weighed heavily on his mind. On the day that the prediction was supposed to come true, he refused to leave his room—the racers were enjoying a rest day. His manager eventually coaxed him out for a drive, and persuaded him to go to a party to help put it out of his mind.

It may have been relief or fear that caused Anquetil to eat and drink more than he should have at that party, but he suffered for it the next day. He was dropped early on the climb of the Port d'Envalira, although he would go on to win the race overall.

The Italian sprinter Mario Cipollini was also said to have believed in psychics. According to Pier Bergonzi of *Gazzetta dello Sport*, this belief dated back to 1994. Prior to the start of that year's Vuelta a España, a psychic named Diamentina, while looking into her crystal ball, saw something that made her fear for Cipollini's safety. She tried to contact him, but could only get through to his brother-in-law. "Mario must not take the start of the race, something terrible is going to happen to him," Diamentina told him.

Unfortunately, Cipollini had already started the race. He was in contention for the stage win that day until his Mercatone Uno teammate Adriano Baffi pushed him against the barriers. He crashed heavily and ended up in a coma. When he emerged, Cipollini was told about Diamantina's prediction, and immediately went to see her. The clairvoyant offered him a small blue lapis lazuli stone that he's been wearing ever since.

The middle-aged lady then started to follow Cipo to races, after he asked her to do so, in a bid to allay his fears. She wasn't the only woman who would be seen trying to meet with the playboy after events, but her reasons were a lot more innocent.

The World Championships and French Championships aren't the only races where bad luck is said to affect the winner. It has also been claimed that winners of one of the season-opening races in France, the Grand Prix d'Ouverture La Marseillaise, go on to have a terrible season. After winning the 2010 event, Frenchman Jonathan Hivert seriously injured his knee in a crash. The winner of the race the previous year, Rémi Pauriol, broke his clavicle in Paris–

Nice shortly afterward, and the winner of the 2007 edition, Jeremy Hunt, struggled even to race that season, as his team Unibet was banned from a lot of events in a clampdown on the advertisement of gambling.

It's not just professional cyclists who believe in superstitions; leisure cyclists also tend to follow strange customs. In recent years, I've seen ads for a company selling a small triangle of wood that can be attached to your handlebars. This is to put your mind at ease in the event that you have a near miss—you can quickly knock on wood. This superstition has lasted the test of time: It's said to date back to pagan times, when knocking on wood was believed to drive out troublesome wood nymphs and protect a person from harm. To cynics like myself, this seems yet another illogical belief, but if it puts people at ease while they race or train, then who are we to knock them?

As we'll see later, though, cycling isn't the only sport that has supposed curses associated with it. As superstitious as professional cyclists might seem, the curse of the rainbow jersey pales into insignificance compared with the strange curses and superstitions in other sports.

17

It's Not Just Cycling

Arguably, the sport associated with the most curses and superstitions is baseball. Many teams have had long losing streaks blamed on particular curses; even individual ballplayers seem to be prone to developing rituals that they feel obligated to follow.

Among the numerous baseball teams said to have been hexed are the Boston Red Sox, Chicago Cubs, and San Francisco Giants. The Curse of the Bambino may be the most famous curse in American sport. Up until 1918, the Red Sox had been one of the most successful professional baseball teams, winning the World Series five times. However, in the off-season of 1919–20, the team sold the legendary Babe Ruth (the Bambino) to the New York Yankees. The Red Sox would subsequently go for years without recapturing the title.

However, it was decades into their streak before anybody even referred to the curse; the first mention only came about in 1990. Following that first reference, the curse seemed to crop up repeatedly whenever the Sox finished yet another season without capturing the World Series. Eventually in 2004, they beat the St. Louis Cardinals to win the title, having beaten their archnemesis, the Yankees, along the way.

"The Curse of the Billy Goat" placed on the Chicago Cubs originated in 1945 when the owner of the Billy Goat Tavern was asked to leave a World Series game against the Detroit Tigers, because the odor from his pet goat was bothering other fans. This tavern owner, Billy Sianis, was supposed to have shouted out, "Them Cubs, they ain't gonna win no more," as he was escorted from the stadium.

Chicago tavern owner Billy Sianis is kicked out of the Chicago Cubs stadium, along with his goat. This incident started "the Curse of the Billy Goat."

Since then, a number of goats have been brought to Wrigley Field in an attempt to break the curse, but nearly seventy years after the incident, the Cubs still haven't won another World Series.

Possibly one of the most bizarre curses is "the "Curse of the Colonel." The Hanshin Tigers, a Japanese baseball team, were supposedly cursed by Colonel Harland Sanders, of all people, the founder of Kentucky Fried Chicken. This came about after a statue of the colonel was tossed into a local river in 1985. The team then went on a losing streak, and it was said that they wouldn't win their championship until the statue was recovered. Numerous attempts were made to find the statue; most of it was eventually recovered twenty-four years later. However, the Tigers' losing streak continues.

Golf has also been affected by superstitions. Since 1960, a pre-tournament event has been organized at the US Masters for the day before the first round. The par-three competition is sandwiched in between practice rounds, and since its inception, no winner of the event has gone on to the win the Masters. It's said that many top golfers deliberately avoid winning the competition.

Another strange sports curse was described in the biography of Australian soccer player Johnny Warren. In the offensively titled *Sheilas, Wogs and Poofters*, Warren describes a trip he made with the national team to Rhodesia in a bid to qualify for the 1970 World Cup. The team visited a witch doctor before its game with Mozambique. The witch doctor buried some animal bones near the goalposts and placed a hex on Mozambique. However, the players struggled to stump up the thousand pounds that he demanded.

When they failed to pay, the witch doctor supposedly placed a curse on the Australian team. The Aussies struggled for the next thirty-six years, until the 2006 World Cup. That was only after another witch doctor had been employed in Mozambique to reverse the curse.

Two soccer teams in England have been cursed for the same reason. Both Derby County and Birmingham City are said to have built stadiums on land used by Romany Gypsies. In revenge, the Gypsies placed curses on both teams. A number of Birmingham's managers tried to lift the curse over the years, including one, Barry Fry, who urinated in all four corners of the pitch after a clairvoyant told him it would break the spell. Fry would later explain why he did it. "We went three months without winning. We were desperate, so I pissed in all four corners, holding it in while I waddled round the pitch," he said in an interview. "Did it work? Well, we started to win and I thought it had, then they fucking sacked me, so probably not."

In the United States, a number of cities have been associated with curses affecting all of their professional sports teams. Cleveland, for example, hasn't won a championship in any major sport since 1964. Buffalo has also struggled over the years.

A strange curse that has emerged in recent years is "the Curse of Aaron Ramsey" or his "Kick of Death," as it has been termed by some. Ramsey is a soccer player with the English team Arsenal. He isn't the most prolific goal scorer, but it has been noticed that whenever he does score a goal, somebody famous dies. Among those who have passed away shortly after Ramsey has scored are Muammar Gaddafi, Steve Jobs, Osama bin Laden, and Whitney Houston.

World-famous figures must be hoping that the Welshman doesn't go on a scoring streak.

The rainbow jersey isn't the only sports jersey apparently cursed. The Dallas Cowboys predominantly play in white, but it is said that their second jersey, colored blue, is jinxed. This myth started after Super Bowl V, and since then, the Cowboys have won just once in a conference championship game when wearing blue—against the Los Angeles Rams in 1978. It has been said that some opposing teams deliberately wear white when playing the Cowboys to force them to wear their blue and therefore invoke the curse.

There is also the famous *Sports Illustrated* curse, which stretches back to the 1950s. The story goes that appearing on the front cover of the magazine has resulted in a downturn of fortune. Among those supposed to have been affected by the curse were the golfer Lee Trevino and boxer Michael Spinks. Trevino was on the cover prior to the US Open in 1969, but subsequently failed to make the cut in the tournament a few days later. Spinks appeared on the cover prior to his fight in 1988 with Mike Tyson with the caption, DON'T COUNT ME OUT. He was promptly knocked out by Tyson in ninety-one seconds and retired from the sport shortly afterward.

The *Sports Illustrated* writer Alexander Wolff decided to determine if there was any truth to this curse. He studied the results of athletes following their appearance on the front cover. Wolff found "a demonstrable misfortune or decline in performance following a cover appearance roughly 37.2 percent of the time." Wolff also reported that almost 12 percent of those on cover suffered injury or death.

These appear to be quite high percentages, suggesting that the hypothesis has been proven. However, Wolff then met with a statistics professor who concluded that the curse is just a "regression to the mean." In other words, the cover stars are usually photographed during a winning streak, and winning streaks eventually come to an end. Also, many of those featuring on the cover went on to become some of the most successful stars in their chosen sports, such as Muhammad Ali and Jack Nicklaus. This can be conveniently overlooked by those propagating the myth.

There are also superstitions completely outside the control of competitors, who can't be affected by them even subconsciously. One example is what's known as "the Commentator's Curse." This refers to the phenomenon whereby a TV or radio commentator talks about how well a particular sports player is performing—only to see the player to spectacularly fail immediately after the comment is made. The particular player involved is of course unaware of the comment, so he can't be affected by it. In reality, this is just coincidental; as with other superstitions, the times when incidents don't align with the myth are forgotten.

So how do superstitions in sport arise? Generally in hindsight. An athlete or observer notices that something the athlete did, or some other event, coincided with a particular result, and attributes the success or failure in performance to the circumstances. Those circumstances may then become a necessary precursor to competition.

A famous example of an athlete associating something he did

with a good performance is Michael Jordan, who wore his University of North Carolina shorts under his Chicago Bulls uniform during every match. This harked back to 1982, when he led UNC to the NCAA Championships, and therefore developed a belief that the shorts had brought him luck.

Multiple Grand Slam–winning tennis player Serena Williams may have the record for developing the most superstitious rituals when playing. Among these are tying her shoelaces in a particular way, and bouncing the ball five times before her first serve, twice before her second; she is also known to wear the same pair of socks throughout a tournament run. She is so superstitious that she often blames exiting a tournament on not following one of her rituals exactly.

The psychologist and founder of the *Psychology of Sports* blog, Dr. Richard Lustberg, explained why athletes such as Williams attribute their success solely to superstition. "If a player has success in sports, it's more than likely because of practice and skill," Lustberg said. "But if the player attributes his or her success to some type of different act, such as wearing a certain article of clothing or repeating some kind of routine, the player will repeat the act. As a result, the player's confidence will rise, and this increased confidence allows the player to perform at a higher level." Unfortunately, this can work both ways, as we've seen.

So cycling is not unique as a sport where superstitions and odd rituals before competition arise. But it's not just sport where these quirks of behavior are seen. They permeate all aspects of everyday life, whether it's avoiding walking under ladders or not spilling salt.

They can play a part in improving your positivity, but you run the risk of becoming too focused on rituals. If a cyclist believes that the rainbow jersey will have a detrimental effect on his performance, then it may well do so.

18

Cursed or Not?

So what exactly constitutes bad luck? I remember watching coverage of the semi-classic E3 Prijs Vlaanderen in spring 2007. World Champion Paolo Bettini was competing, and he could be expected to do well. On the climb of the Knokteberg, however, his rear derailleur broke. The commentator said something to the effect that the curse had struck again. I felt that this was really stretching the effects of the superstition too far. E3 Prijs could hardly be considered among the biggest races, and a broken derailleur wouldn't be considered a tragedy. These things happen.

Cycling is a dangerous sport, and the vast majority of professionals will crash during a particular season, whether they are wearing the World Champion's jersey or not. There is just more focus on the incident when you are wearing the jersey. You could randomly select the holder of any other title in the sport, and compile a list of the unfortunate events that he suffered in the year after his win. If you were to consider reigning Tour de France champions and the misfortunes they have suffered in the subsequent seasons, the list would be considerable. Among the bad-luck incidents encountered by Tour winners are being accidentally shot, suffering numerous injuries, and getting caught doping. Yet nobody ever speaks of a curse of the Tour winner.

It can also be easily forgotten that winning the rainbow jersey resulted in some riders going on to have their best-ever seasons. Bernard Hinault won what was arguably the toughest Worlds ever in Sallanches in 1980. He went on to win Paris–Roubaix, Amstel Gold, and the Tour de France the following season. Giuseppe Saronni was the winner in 1982; the year afterward, he had his best season ever as he won Milan–San Remo, the Giro d'Italia, and the Tour of Lombardy. Following his win in 2005, Tom Boonen went on to win twenty-one races the next season, including the Tour of Flanders.

Other World Champions have gone on to have great years in the rainbow jersey, including Bernard Hinault, the 1980 World Champion.

It's worth looking at whether some World Champions may be affected by a variation on the nocebo effect. The nocebo effect is the opposite of the better-known placebo effect. In essence, what it means in medical terms is that if a patient is given a dummy drug and is told, or believes, that it will be harmful, then the patient will report a deterioration in health.

Like the placebo effect, the nocebo works through a psychological response rather than a physical. If patients are particularly pessimistic, then there will be an increased likelihood that they will report a worsening of their health. Have some cyclists been affected by something similar? If somebody is told that wearing a particular jersey will result in him having a poor year, then he might. However, it depends on the character of the rider. If Nico Mattan or Jacques Anquetil had been World Champion, then he quite possibly might have succumbed to the belief that he would suffer accordingly. Still, many former World Champions have been dismissive of the curse when asked about particularly bad performances.

The more common term for this type of effect would be *self-fulfilling prophecy*. A self-fulfilling prophecy has been defined in the Thomas theorem—a sociological theorem—thusly: "If men define situations as real, they are real in their consequences." In other words, the way in which a situation is interpreted will cause the action to take place. A classic example was the Oil Crisis of 1973. Following an embargo by the members of OPEC, rumors started that there would be a shortage of toilet paper due to problems with the importation of oil. This resulted in people stockpiling toilet paper, thus creating a shortage.

Sports psychology has grown more and more important in the past few years, with the British Team Sky among a growing number of teams to employ a sports psychiatrist. Dr. Steve Peters helps the team's riders understand how the individual's mind works and how this can help maximize performance. The use of sports psychology is also growing in other sports.

The Spanish soccer team employed a Boston University professor and director of sports psychology training, Leonard Zaichkowsky, prior to the 2006 World Cup. He was tasked with getting team members to start thinking like champions. Despite having some of the best players in the world, the team had been underachieving for decades. Its only tournament success had been in 1964. It didn't win the World Cup in 2006, but shortly afterward it started a thirty-five-match undefeated streak. Since then it has gone on to win the European Championships twice and the 2010 World Cup.

The media obviously help propagate the myth of the rainbow jersey. As soon as a new World Champion suffers his first misfortune (as with Philippe Gilbert's crash in the 2012 Giro di Lombardia), references are made to the curse, regardless of how small the misfortune was. Television cameramen are also more likely to focus their attention on the World Champion standing at the side of the road with a puncture than they are on another cyclist. The 2011 World Champion Mark Cavendish remarked that anytime he was getting dropped on a climb in a race, TV cameras seemed to focus on him more than others. He felt the burden of wearing the jersey at the start of the following season, saying, "This season has been the first time in my career when I've consistently been marked, when I've consistently felt that it's not been about someone else winning—it's about me not being there. I'm not the first guy to get dropped usually; there are other guys who get dropped before me, but the TV camera is usually on me."

The 2005 World Champion Tom Boonen was one rider who dismissed talk of any curse, believing that poor performance was purely psychological. When asked about the curse, he said, "The rainbow curse is something that doesn't exist. If you're able to win the World Championships, you can win other races as well. What comes with the rainbow jersey is pressure, and if you're good with pressure, you can deal with the rainbow jersey."

When asked about his bad luck in the 2011 Paris–Roubaix, then reigning World Champion Thor Hushovd was also dismissive of the curse, and was even more forthright than Boonen in denying its existence. "It's time to stop harping on the damn curse," he responded angrily to one reporter's question. "There is no curse of the World Champion jersey, and there is no curse here in Roubaix."

It could be also be considered that belief in the curse is an example of confirmation bias—the phenomenon whereby, decision makers seek out and assign more weight to evidence that confirms their hypothesis. In this instance, believers in the curse will cite Jean-Pierre Monseré and Freddy Maertens as curse victims while neglecting to mention those wearers who have had great subsequent seasons such as Tom Boonen. For cycling journalists discussing another unfortunate victim of the curse, the writing task is easier if they focus on evidence consistent with their hypothesis.

The results of one interesting study undertaken on sports psychology were published in *Psychological Science*. As part of the experiment, golf balls were given to all of the subjects. Half of the participants were told that their golf ball was lucky, and these subjects made 35 percent more successful putts. Feeling lucky gave them a better sense of self-efficacy (a belief in your own competence), which then enhanced their performance playing golf.

So it would seem that a cyclist's awareness of the supposed curse may in some instances be detrimental to his performance. A professor of psychology at Connecticut College, Dr. Stuart Vyse, explained this negative effect: "I don't see any benefit to teaching people the unlucky superstitions—the number 13, black cats, and so forth—these are superstitions that merely increase anxiety and force you into situations where if it comes along you have to think about whether or not you want to deal with it." This would suggest that if a World Champion was oblivious to the curse on the jersey he'd just won, he might go on to perform better.

Although it is unlikely that any rational-thinking cyclist would think this way, another consideration for a rainbow jersey wearer is that should he suffer any sort of misfortune, it would be a mistake to blame it on the jersey. The sports performance coach Jeremy Lazarus has warned against attributing a poor performance to bad luck, which can be counterproductive and put you in a negative mind-set. "While this may be an unfortunate occurrence," Lazarus said, "if you have mentally prepared and planned for any problems, then such incidents shouldn't affect your concentration or attitude."

It's difficult to determine if there is any substance to the curse—more specifically, whether there is a downturn in performance after winning the title. Quite a few variables are involved: Some wins are more important than others, for example, and World Champions also do a great job of helping team members in ways that are not recognized on their palmarès. However, I'm going to try to add some objectivity to the discussion. If we start from 1955, and look at the results for each rider before and after winning the Worlds, it may help us determine whether winning the jersey leads to a slide in results.

Of the fifty-seven winners from Stan Ockers in 1955 up to and including Mark Cavendish in 2011, six riders have won as many races while wearing the rainbow jersey as they did in the year leading up to their title win. Twenty-eight riders have had a better subsequent season, while twenty-three have gone on to have a worse year. So nearly 60 percent of riders go on to have an equal or better season after winning the Worlds. This calculation alone suggests that there is no such thing as a curse.

As a comparison, I looked at another top race, Paris–Roubaix, to see if the winners of the cobbled classic went on to have more or less successful subsequent seasons. Once again, I compared the results of winners from 1955 onward. Sixteen winners would go on to have a more successful season after taking winning in Roubaix, while five would have an equally successful season. Therefore, only 37 percent of Paris–Roubaix winners would go on to have an equal or better subsequent season, compared with 60 percent of World Champions. All this might suggest that there should be a "curse of the Paris–Roubaix winner." It's not as catchy, though.

Finally, I looked at the statistics from the Tour de France from the same time frame. Less than 27 percent of Tour winners would go on to have an equal or better season after taking the title. There is less Tour data to work with for the time period, however, due to a certain cyclist being stripped of his seven titles. So it seems that if you must choose one race to win—Paris–Roubaix, the Tour de France, or the World Championships—to ensure that you have a good follow-on season, then the Worlds is your best bet.

Yet it seems likely that talk of the curse of the rainbow jersey will rumble on for years. Unlike other curses that can be "broken" by a team ending a losing streak or finally winning that elusive championship, somebody is always going to win the World Championships and go on to struggle or suffer some misfortune, no matter how small. The next time you see the new World Champion at the side of the road with a puncture, you can guarantee that the curse will be at the forefront of the minds of cycling journalists and fans alike.

Appendix: World Championship Results

Championships	Gold	Silver	Bronze
1927 Nürburgring	Alfredo Binda (ITA)	Costante Girardengo (ITA)	Domenico Piemontesi (ITA)
1928 Budapest	Georges Ronsse (BEL)	Herbert Nebe (GER)	Bruno Wolke (GER)
1929 Zürich	Georges Ronsse (BEL)	Nicolas Frantz (LUX)	Alfredo Binda (ITA)
1930 Liège	Alfredo Binda (ITA)	Learco Guerra (ITA)	Georges Ronsse (BEL)
1931 Copenhagen	Learco Guerra (ITA)	Ferdinand Le Drogo (FRA)	Albert Büchi (SUI)
1932 Rome	Alfredo Binda (ITA)	Remo Bertoni (ITA)	Nicolas Frantz (LUX)
1933 Montlhéry	Georges Speicher (FRA)	Antonin Magne (FRA)	Marinus Valentijn (NED)
1934 Leipzig	Karel Kaers (BEL)	Learco Guerra (ITA)	Gustave Danneels (BEL)
1935 Floreffe	Jean Aerts (BEL)	Luciano Montero (ESP)	Gustave Danneels (BEL)
1936 Bern	Antonin Magne (FRA)	Aldo Bini (ITA)	Theo Middelkamp (NED)
1937 Copenhagen	Eloi Meulenberg (BEL)	Emil Kijewski (GER)	Paul Egli (SUI)
1938 Valkenburg	Marcel Kint (BEL)	Paul Egli (SUI)	Leo Amberg (SUI)
1946 Zürich	Hans Knecht (SUI)	Marcel Kint (BEL)	Rik Van Steenbergen (BEL)
1947 Reims	Theo Middelkamp (NED)	Albert Sercu (BEL)	Sjef Janssen (NED)
1948 Valkenburg	Briek Schotte (BEL)	Apo Lazarides (FRA)	Lucien Teisseire (FRA)
1949 Copenhagen	Rik Van Steenbergen (BEL)	Ferdi Kübler (SUI)	Fausto Coppi (ITA)
1950 Moorslede	Briek Schotte (BEL)	Theo Middelkamp (NED)	Ferdi Kübler (SUI)
1951 Varese	Ferdi Kübler (SUI)	Fiorenzo Magni (ITA)	Antonio Bevilacqua (ITA)
1952 Luxembourg	Heinz Müller (FRG)	Gottfried Weilemann (SUI)	Ludwig Hormann (FRG)
1953 Lugano	Fausto Coppi (ITA)	Germain Derycke (BEL)	Stan Ockers (BEL)

Year	Venue	1st	2nd	3rd
1954	Solingen	Louison Bobet (FRA)	Fritz Schaer (SUI)	Charly Gaul (LUX)
1955	Frascati	Stan Ockers (BEL)	Jean-Pierre Schmitz (LUX)	Germain Derycke (BEL)
1956	Copenhagen	Rik Van Steenbergen (BEL)	Rik van Looy (BEL)	Gerrit Schulte (NED)
1957	Waregem	Rik Van Steenbergen (BEL)	Louison Bobet (FRA)	André Darrigade (FRA)
1958	Reims	Ercole Baldini (ITA)	Louison Bobet (FRA)	André Darrigade (FRA)
1959	Zandvoort	André Darrigade (FRA)	Michele Gismondi (ITA)	Noël Foré (BEL)
1960	Karl-Marx-Stadt	Rik van Looy (BEL)	André Darrigade (FRA)	Pino Cerami (BEL)
1961	Bern	Rik van Looy (BEL)	Nino Defilippis (ITA)	Raymond Poulidor (FRA)
1962	Salò di Garda	Jean Stablinski (FRA)	Seamus Elliott (IRL)	Jos Hoevenaers (BEL)
1963	Ronse	Benoni Beheyt (BEL)	Rik van Looy (BEL)	Jo de Haan (NED)
1964	Sallanches	Jan Janssen (NED)	Vittorio Adorni (ITA)	Raymond Poulidor (FRA)
1965	San Sebastián	Tom Simpson (GBR)	Rudi Altig (FRG)	Roger Swerts (BEL)
1966	Nürburgring	Rudi Altig (FRG)	Jacques Anquetil (FRA)	Raymond Poulidor (FRA)
1967	Heerlen	Eddy Merckx (BEL)	Jan Janssen (NED)	Ramón Sáez (ESP)
1968	Imola	Vittorio Adorni (ITA)	Herman van Springel (BEL)	Michele Dancelli (ITA)
1969	Zolder	Harm Ottenbros (NED)	Julien Stevens (BEL)	Michele Dancelli (ITA)
1970	Leicester	Jean-Pierre Monseré (BEL)	Leif Mortensen (DEN)	Felice Gimondi (ITA)
1971	Mendrisio	Eddy Merckx (BEL)	Felice Gimondi (ITA)	Cyrille Guimard (FRA)
1972	Gap	Marino Basso (ITA)	Franco Bitossi (ITA)	Cyrille Guimard (FRA)
1973	Barcelona	Felice Gimondi (ITA)	Freddy Maertens (BEL)	Luis Ocaña (ESP)
1974	Montreal	Eddy Merckx (BEL)	Raymond Poulidor (FRA)	Mariano Martínez (FRA)
1975	Yvoir	Hennie Kuiper (NED)	Roger de Vlaeminck (BEL)	Jean-Pierre Danguillaume (FRA)
1976	Ostuni	Freddy Maertens (BEL)	Francesco Moser (ITA)	Tino Conti (ITA)
1977	San Cristóbal	Francesco Moser (ITA)	Dietrich Thurau (FRG)	Franco Bitossi (ITA)
1978	Nürburgring	Gerrie Knetemann (NED)	Francesco Moser (ITA)	Jörgen Marcussen (DEN)

185

Championships	Gold	Silver	Bronze
1979 Valkenburg	Jan Raas (NED)	Dietrich Thurau (FRG)	Jean-René Bernaudeau (FRA)
1980 Sallanches	Bernard Hinault (FRA)	Gianbattista Baronchelli (ITA)	Juan Fernández (ESP)
1981 Brno	Freddy Maertens (BEL)	Giuseppe Saronni (ITA)	Bernard Hinault (FRA)
1982 Goodwood	Giuseppe Saronni (ITA)	Greg LeMond (USA)	Sean Kelly (IRL)
1983 Altenrhein	Greg LeMond (USA)	Adri van der Poel (NED)	Stephen Roche (IRL)
1984 Barcelona	Claude Criquielion (BEL)	Claudio Corti (ITA)	Steve Bauer (CAN)
1985 Giavera del Montello	Joop Zoetemelk (NED)	Greg LeMond (USA)	Moreno Argentin (ITA)
1986 Colorado Springs	Moreno Argentin (ITA)	Charly Mottet (FRA)	Giuseppe Saronni (ITA)
1987 Villach	Stephen Roche (IRL)	Moreno Argentin (ITA)	Juan Fernández (ESP)
1988 Ronse	Maurizio Fondriest (ITA)	Martial Gayant (FRA)	Juan Fernández (ESP)
1989 Chambéry	Greg LeMond (USA)	Dimitri Konychev (URS)	Sean Kelly (IRL)
1990 Utsunomiya	Rudy Dhaenens (BEL)	Dirk De Wolf (BEL)	Gianni Bugno (ITA)
1991 Stuttgart	Gianni Bugno (ITA)	Steven Rooks (NED)	Miguel Induráin (ESP)
1992 Benidorm	Gianni Bugno (ITA)	Laurent Jalabert (FRA)	Dimitri Konychev (RUS)
1993 Oslo	Lance Armstrong (USA)	Miguel Indurain (ESP)	Olaf Ludwig (GER)
1994 Agrigento	Luc Leblanc (FRA)	Claudio Chiappucci (ITA)	Richard Virenque (FRA)
1995 Duitama	Abraham Olano (ESP)	Miguel Induráin (ESP)	Marco Pantani (ITA)
1996 Lugano	Johan Museeuw (BEL)	Mauro Gianetti (SUI)	Michele Bartoli (ITA)
1997 San Sebastián	Laurent Brochard (FRA)	Bo Hamburger (DEN)	Léon van Bon (NED)
1998 Valkenburg	Oscar Camenzind (SUI)	Peter Van Petegem (BEL)	Michele Bartoli (ITA)
1999 Verona	Óscar Freire (ESP)	Markus Zberg (SUI)	Jean-Cyril Robin (FRA)
2000 Plouay	Rom ns Vainšteins (LAT)	Zbigniew Spruch (POL)	Óscar Freire (ESP)

Year	Location	Winner	Second	Third
2001	Lisbon	Óscar Freire (ESP)	Paolo Bettini (ITA)	Andrej Hauptman (SLO)
2002	Zolder/Hasselt	Mario Cipollini (ITA)	Robbie McEwen (AUS)	Erik Zabel (GER)
2003	Hamilton	Igor Astarloa (ESP)	Alejandro Valverde (ESP)	Peter Van Petegem (BEL)
2004	Verona	Óscar Freire (ESP)	Erik Zabel (GER)	Luca Paolini (ITA)
2005	Madrid	Tom Boonen (BEL)	Alejandro Valverde (ESP)	Anthony Geslin (FRA)
2006	Salzburg	Paolo Bettini (ITA)	Erik Zabel (GER)	Alejandro Valverde (ESP)
2007	Stuttgart	Paolo Bettini (ITA)	Alexandr Kolobnev (RUS)	Stefan Schumacher (GER)
2008	Varese	Alessandro Ballan (ITA)	Damiano Cunego (ITA)	Matti Breschel (DEN)
2009	Mendrisio	Cadel Evans (AUS)	Alexandr Kolobnev (RUS)	Joaquim Rodríguez (ESP)
2010	Geelong	Thor Hushovd (NOR)	Matti Breschel (DEN)	Allan Davis (AUS)
2011	Copenhagen	Mark Cavendish (GBR)	Matthew Goss (AUS)	André Greipel (GER)
2012	Valkenburg	Philippe Gilbert (BEL)	Edvald Boasson Hagen (NOR)	Alejandro Valverde (ESP)

Bibliography

Books

Coyle, D., *Lance Armstrong's War: One Man's Battle Against Fate, Fame, Love, Death, Scandal, and a Few Other Rivals on the Road to the Tour de France* (Harper Paperbacks, 2010).

Fotheringham, W., *Put Me Back on My Bike* (Yellow Jersey Press, 2002).

Maertens, F., *Fall from Grace* (Ronde Publications, 1993).

Newton, N., and B. Minutaglio, *Locker Room Mojo: True Tales of Superstitions in Sports* (Middlefork Press, 1999).

Roche, S., *Born to Ride* (Yellow Jersey Press, 2012).

————, *My Road to Victory* (Stanley Paul, 1988).

Roche, S., & D. Walsh, *The Agony and the Ecstasy: Stephen Roche's World of Cycling* (Stanley Paul, 1988).

Sidwells, C., *Mr. Tom: The True Story of Tom Simpson* (Mousehold Press, 2000).

Simpson, T., *Cycling Is my Life* (Yellow Jersey Press, 2009).

Voet, W., *Breaking the Chain: Drugs and Cycling: The True Story* (Yellow Jersey Press, 2001).

Warren, J., *Sheilas, Wogs and Poofters* (Random House Australia, 2003).

Woodland, L., *The Yellow Jersey Companion to the Tour de France* (Yellow Jersey Press, 2003).

Magazines and Newspapers

Bicisport
Cycle Sport
Cycling Weekly
Daily Telegraph

Der Spiegel
France-Soir
Gazet van Antwerpen
Gazzetta dello Sport
Het Laatse Nieuws
L'Équipe
Marca
New York Times
Procycling
Psychological Science
Sports Illustrated
The Guardian
The Observer
The People
USA Today

Websites

www.bbc.co.uk
www.cyclingnews.com
www.cyclingrevelealed.com
www.dailypeloton.com
www.insideworldsoccer.com
www.pezcyclingnews.com
www.psychologyofsports.com
www.sbnation.com
www.sportkroniek.nl

Graham Healy is a keen cyclist and author from Dublin, Ireland. This is his second book, having previously written a biography of an Irish cyclist, *Shay Elliott: The Life and Death of Ireland's First Yellow Jersey.*

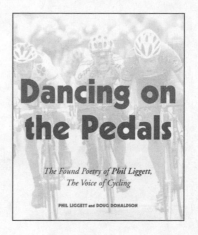

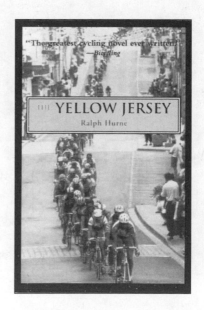

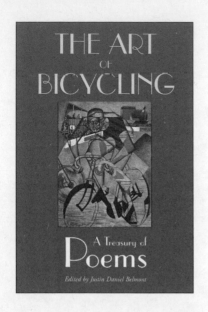

THE ART OF BICYCLING

A Treasury of Poems

Edited by Justin Daniel Belmont

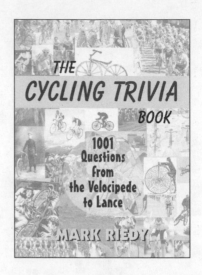

THE CYCLING TRIVIA BOOK

1001 Questions from the Velocipede to Lance

MARK RIEDY

The Long Season

BRUNO SCHULL

BICYCLE LOVE

STORIES OF PASSION, JOY, AND SWEAT